The Sneeze

PLAYS AND STORIES BY

Anton Chekhov

TRANSLATED AND ADAPTED BY

Michael Frayn

SAMUEL FRENCH, INC.

45 WEST 25TH STREET   NEW YORK 10010
7623 SUNSET BOULEVARD   HOLLYWOOD 90046
LONDON   TORONTO

Contents

4

Anton Pavlovich Chekhov

1860 Born the son of a grocer and grandson of a serf, in Taganrog, a small port on the Sea of Azov, where he spends his first nineteen years, and which he describes on a return visit in later life as 'Asia, pure and simple!'

1875 His father, bankrupt, flees from Taganrog concealed beneath a mat at the bottom of a cart.

1876 A former lodger buys the Chekhovs' house and puts the rest of the family out.

1879 Chekhov rejoins his family, who have followed his father to Moscow, and enrols at the university to study medicine.

1880 Begins contributing humorous material to minor magazines under the pen-name Antosha Chekhonte.

1882 Begins contributing regularly to the St Petersburg humorous journal *Oskolki*—short stories and sketches, and a column on Moscow life.

1884 Qualifies as a doctor, and begins practising in Moscow—the start of a sporadic second career which over the years brings him much hard work but little income.

1885 Begins writing for the *St Petersburg Gazette*, which gives him the opportunity to break out of the tight restrictions on length and the rigidly humorous format in which he has worked up to now.

1886 Another step up the journalistic ladder—he begins writing, under his own name and for good money, for *Novoye vremya*. Alexei Suvorin, its millionaire proprietor, an anti-Semitic reactionary who had the concession on all the railway bookstands in Russia, becomes Chekhov's close friend.

1887 Is a literary success in St Petersburg. Writes *Ivanov* as a result of a commission from a producer who wants a light entertainment in the Chekhonte style. The play is produced in Moscow (his first production) to a mixture of clapping and hissing.

1888 Begins to publish his stories in the 'thick journals'; has survived his career in comic journalism to emerge as a serious and respectable writer. But at the same time begins writing four one-act farces for the theatre.

1889 *The Wood Demon* (which Chekhov later uses as raw material for *Uncle Vanya*) opens at a second-rate Moscow theatre, and survives for only three performances.

1890 Makes the appalling journey across Siberia (largely in unsprung carts over unsurfaced roads) to visit and report on the penal colony on the island of Sakhalin. Sets out to interview the entire population of prisoners and exiles, at the rate of 160 a day.

1892 Travels the back country of Nizhny Novgorod and Voronyezh provinces in the middle of winter, trying to prevent a recurrence of the previous years's famine among the peasants. Is banqueted by the provincial governors. Moves to the modest but comfortable estate he had bought himself at Melikhovo, fifty miles south of Moscow. Becomes an energetic and enlightened landowner, cultivating the soil and doctoring the peasants. Spends three months organizing the district against an expected cholera epidemic.

1894 Starts work on the first of the three schools he builds in the Melikhovo district.

1896 *The Seagull* opens in St Petersburg, and survives only five performances after a disastrous first night. Chekhov tells Suvorin he won't have another play put on even if he lives another seven hundred years.

1897 Suffers a violent lung haemorrhage while dining with Suvorin, and is forced to recognize at last what he has long closed his eyes to—that he is suffering from advanced consumption. (Is also constantly plagued by piles, gastritis, migraine, dizzy spells, and palpitations of the heart.) Winters in Nice.

1898 Moves his headquarters to the Crimean warmth of Yalta. Stanislavsky revives *The Seagull* (with twelve weeks rehearsal) at the newly-founded Moscow Arts Theatre, and it is an immediate success.

1899 Sells the copyright in all his works, past, present, and future, to the St Petersburg publisher A.F. Marks—a contract which is to burden the rest of his life. *Uncle Vanya* produced successfully by the Moscow Arts Theatre.

1901 *Three Sisters* produced by the Moscow Arts Theatre, but rather poorly received. Chekhov marries his mistress, Olga Knipper, an actress in the Moscow Arts company, the original Arkadina in *The Seagull*, Yelena in *Uncle Vanya*, Masha in *Three Sisters* and Ranyevskaya in *The Cherry Orchard*.

1904 *The Cherry Orchard* is produced in January; and in July, after two heart attacks, Chekhov dies in a hotel bedroom in the German spa of Badenweiler.

Introduction

The word 'Chekhovian' has been applied, with generous imprecision, to a fair number of things in this world; but probably never, even in its vaguest sense, to Chekhov's own one-act plays. They are in a different mode from the four great dramas that constitute the Chekhovian in most people's minds; they are offered not as part but as entertainment. The best of them are (for the greater part) straightforwardly comic. Chekhov, of course, first made his reputation as a humorist, but these plays are surprising because they were mostly written in the late 1880s, when he was approaching the age of thirty—precisely when he had escaped from the limitations of humorous writing, and was just beginning to be taken seriously as a literary writer. In fact his two careers, in literature and in the theatre, were quite distinct, and oddly out of step with each other from the very beginning. What happened in the late eighties is that the careers switched tracks. In one and the same year, 1888, the successful boulevard journalist became accepted as a writer of serious fiction, and the unsuccessful serious dramatist emerged as a writer of popular boulevard comedies.

It was the publication in that year of his long story *The Steppe* which established his literary reputation. It marked the culmination of a decade in which flippant spoofs and skits in the comic journals had quite slowly matured into stories of the most exquisite restraint and profound insight. But he had been writing serious and substantial work for the theatre from the very beginning, starting with the huge untitled drama of his student days. This was followed in 1885 by a long one-act play entitled *On the Highroad*, which is probably melodrama, but which attempts a striking picture of society's lower

7

depths. Neither of these was performed during his life-
time. The former was supposedly torn up after its rejec-
tion, and did not resurface until sixteen years after Chekhov's death, while the latter he seems to have abandoned
after it was forbidden by the censor as being 'too gloomy
and sordid', and also, to judge by the underlining in the
censor's report, because it showed a member of the
landowning classes in a drunken and destitute condi-
tion. His first seriously-intended work of any length to
come before the public (leaving aside his detective novel,
The Shooting Party, which, for all its delicious brilliance,
was written as a pot-boiler) was also a play — *Ivanov*, in
1887. It was written (in ten days, according to Chekhov)
at the suggestion of the theatre-manager Korsh. Korsh
specialised in light comedy, and Chekhov's sister Masha
said he threw out his proposal — rather casually, according to her, during a conversation in the foyer of the
theatre — because of Chekhov's reputation as a humorist. He apparently did not blench when he received the
resulting script; though Chekhov did when he saw
Korsh's production of it. There were four rehearsals instead of the promised ten, and on the opening night only
two of the cast knew their parts; the rest got through, said
Chekhov, 'by prompter and inner conviction'. The re-
views were decidedly mixed. So were the reactions of the
first-night audience. According to Masha afterwards
people kept jumping to their feet. 'Some clapped, some
hissed and loudly whistled, others stamped their feet.
The chairs and seats in the stalls got moved out of place
and the rows got all mixed up and pushed together, so
that you couldn't find your seat afterwards; the people
sitting in the boxes grew alarmed, and didn't know
whether to go or stay. And as for what was going on in the
gallery — it defies imagination; absolute carnage broke

out up there between the hissers and the clappers.' As a dramatist he had to wait another ten years, with the second production of *The Seagull* at the Moscow Arts Theatre, before he was taken seriously.

In the meantime he adapted his talents as a humorist to the requirements of the stage. A number of his early comic pieces had been in dialogue form, and the short plays he now began to write are in some ways a natural extension of the genre. He had made his first attempt two years before *Ivanov* with a monologue, *The Evils of Tobacco* (signed, like his old comic pieces, 'Antosha Chekhonte'). He intended this 'in the secrecy of his heart' for performance, but in the event it was published in a collection of his stories, and seems not to have been performed until fifteen years later. It was the next one, *Swan Song*, that gave him his first small success in the theatre. He adapted it from one of his stories (*Calchas*), and it was produced at Korsh's just after *Ivanov*. It was merely part of a mixed bill, but it was a vastly more suitable piece for the house, and it was well enough received for proposals to be made for remounting it at the Maly, one of the imperial theatres. It must have seemed clear where his future in the theatre lay, and in the same month he was already writing another short play (an original one this time)— *The Bear*. He subtitled it 'a joke in one act', and it was indeed a comedy pure and simple, with none of the pathos of *Swan Song*. When it was done at Korsh's the following year (six months after the publication of *The Steppe*) it immediately established him as one of the leading boulevard playwrights of the day. Chekhov complained that he and his sister could have acted better than the cast at Korsh's (though he dedicated the play to Solovtsov, who played the lead), and the run nearly ended after the first night when the leading lady was scalded in the face by an exploding coffee-pot. But it made the audience laugh non-stop, and by the following year another commercial management, Abramova's, was fighting Korsh for the rights. It went on to cause a 'furore' (according to the writer Pleshcheyev) at the Alexandrinsky, the imperial theatre in St Petersburg, and then to take the provinces by storm. Chekhov found it being played in several of the Siberian towns he passed through on his way to Sakhalin in 1890. It became such a favourite of amateur dramatic groups that Chekhov was complaining a decade later that 'practically every lady I meet begins her acquaintance with me by saying: "I've acted in your *Bear*!"' And Tolstoy, who thought all Chekhov's later plays were even worse than Shakespeare's, was reported by Olga Knipper to have laughed until he could laugh no more.

Chekhov followed this up the same year with another one-act 'joke' in much the same vein, *The Proposal*. He expressed some doubts about this one. In a letter to the writer Shcheglov he said that he had 'knocked it together specifically for the provinces'. It would pass muster there, he thought, but he did not propose to put it on in the capital. It was in fact successfully performed in Moscow at the Maly, and given in St Petersburg before the Tsar, who was moved to send the author his compliments. Over the next few years Chekhov wrote four more short plays. One of them, *Tatyana Repina*, is a parody of a drama by his wealthy publisher friend Suvorin, and seems to have been intended purely for Suvorin's amusement. It makes insufficient sense without a knowledge of the original on which it was based, but it is striking in its counterpointing of an endless Orthodox marriage service with the scandalised comments of the congregation when they realise that the bridegroom's abandoned mistress, who has supposedly poisoned herself, is present in the church. There is also a wonderful old watchman at the church who dismisses the whole idea of weddings. 'Every day they go marrying and christening and burying, and there's no sense in any of it . . . They sing, they burn incense, they read, and God never listens. Forty years I've worked here, and not once did God ever listen . . . And where this God is I don't know . . . There's no point in any of it . . .' The other three one-act plays from this period, *The Reluctant Tragedian, The Wedding,* and *The Anniversary* (together with a fourth, *The Night before the Trial,* which he left unfinished) were all adapted from his old stories. They had a less striking success than their predecessors. Even so, *The Wedding* made Tolstoy 'collapse with laughter' (as reported by Olga Knipper, at any rate), and *The Anniversary,* when it was finally performed in St Petersburg over a decade later, to mixed notices, still had the audience, according to one critic, 'not so much laughing as simply rolling with laughter.'

Chekhov designated most of the one-act comedies on their title-pages as 'jokes', and consistently disparages them all in his letters. *The Proposal,* he said, was 'a mangy little vaudeville'. *The Bear* was 'a piffling little Frenchified vaudeville' which he had written because he had nothing better to do, having used up so much 'sap and energy' on *The Steppe* that he was incapable of doing anything serious for a long time afterwards. When, in later years, Olga Knipper reported that Stanislavsky was interested in the rewritten version of *The Evils of Tobacco,* Chekhov was so appalled at the idea of 'doing a vaudeville at the Arts Theatre' that he wrote back to her saying she had gone mad, and adding three exclamation marks. He claimed to have dashed these wretched 'vaudevilles' off at odd moments. He had ruined *The Evils of Tobacco*, he said, because he had only two-and-a-half hours to write it in. *Swan Song* he claimed to have written in one hour five minutes. The work on the latter, of course, involved mostly just transcription from an existing story, but even so it at least challenges the record playwriting speeds credited to Noël Coward and Alan Ayckbourn, each of whom is said to have written a full-length original play in three days. If Chekhov could have maintained his claimed rate with original material over the full course he would have completed *Hay Fever* or *Absurd Person Singular* inside a single working day.

Still, at the time he wrote most of these plays he was going through a phase of hating the theatre altogether. In his letter to Shcheglov about *The Proposal* he urged him to give up his love-affair with the stage. The modern theatre, he told him, was 'the venereal disease of the cities'. In fact a letter to another writer, Bezhetzky, suggests that he regarded 'vaudevilles' as a slightly less pathological manifestation than other types of play. 'I don't like the theatre,' he told him, 'I quickly get bored — but I do like watching vaudevilles.' With characteristic self-mocking jauntiness he said he also believed in vaudevilles as an author, and that 'anyone in possession of fifty acres and ten tolerable vaudevilles I reckon to be a made man — his widow will never die of hunger.' If a vaudeville turned out badly, he urged Bezhetzky, 'don't be bashful — just stick a pen-name on it. The provinces will swallow anything. Just try to see there are good parts. The simpler the setting and the smaller the cast, the more often the vaudeville will be done.' The cynical tone is no doubt all part of the flippant pose, but the content is hard-headed, practical advice (as true now, incidentally, as it was then) that he was following himself. It was offered only a month before urging Shcheglov to flee the theatrical pox; and only a month after the Shcheglov letter he was telling Suvorin that he was going to turn to vaudevilles when he had written himself out in other directions. 'I think I could write them at the rate of a hundred a year. Ideas for vaudevilles pour out of me like oil from the Baku wells.' He even wondered whether he shouldn't donate his 'stake in the oilfield' to Shcheglov.

It has to be admitted, I think, that Chekhov's vaudevilles are of somewhat mixed quality. *The Reluctant Tragedian* is thin and facetious; *The Wedding* is a laboured and rather patronising joke on lower middle-class social pretension; *The Anniversary* is repetitive and contrived; *The Night before the Trial* is in a well-worn tradition of comedy about cuckolded husbands. But the four I have chosen for this collection have solid theatrical virtues. *The Evils of Tobacco* and *Swan Song* both touch upon some deeper desolation than boulevard plays normally care to show; the old actor gazing forlornly into the blackness of the empty theatre, and the wretched lecturer who is not so much hen-pecked as hen-eaten and left as droppings, have something in common with Gogol's Poprishchin and Akaky Akakiyevich. And *The Bear* and *The Proposal* are classics of the comic theatre, full of energy, invention, and actors' opportunities. They are larger than life, certainly, but splendid in their magnification. Chekhov's designation for them both, 'joke', is usually translated into English as 'farce'. The term is of course as capacious as 'Chekhovian', but there is a considerable difference between these plays and most French or English farces. As we know the form it usually depends upon panic, and the panic is usually generated by guilt and the prospect of some kind of social disgrace. The panic leads in its turn to deceit, which produces further and yet more alarming prospects of disgrace, from which grows ever greater panic, in a spiral known to scientists as positive feedback. There is no panic in *The Bear* or *The Proposal*, no deceit or threatened disgrace. What drives these characters is a sense of outrage—of anger at the failure of others to recognise their claims, whether to money or to land or to a certain status. In their anger, it is true, they lose the ability to control their destinies or even to recognise their own best interests, just as the characters of traditional farce do in their panic. This is what these plays have in common with English and French farces—that there characters are reduced by their passions to the level of blind and inflexible machines; though this reduction is precisely what Bergson thought (implausibly, to my mind) was the common factor in all comedy.

Chekhov may well have taken his vaudevilles more seriously than his offhandedness about them suggests. He was, after all, notably flippant about *The Seagull*, but there is no doubt that he felt deeply about it. However quickly and cynically he claimed to have written his short plays, he took considerable care over correcting and improving them in the various published editions through which they subsequently went. He lavished particular care upon *The Evils of Tobacco*. Even if he spent only two-and-a-half hours, as he claimed, on the original version, he must have spent many times more than that on the later ones. Over the years the piece went through six major revisions. The last of them was almost at the end of his life, in 1902, when he was writing *The Cherry Orchard*. This was so radical that he claimed the result as an entirely new play, and indeed the whole tone of the piece, if not the substance, had certainly changed considerably by this time. By the sixth edition the comedy has

largely drained away, and left the hapless Nyukhin without the snuff-taking that presumably first gave him his
name (Sniff), but with a confession of despair now as
stark and unconcealed in its way as Uncle Vanya's or
Andrey Prozorov's.

In fact one of the liberties I have taken in this collection is to restore some of the humour of the earlier ver-
sions of this particular play. I have used the final edition
of 1902 as the basis of my text, and Nyukhin reaches his
direct confession of despair at the end, but on the way to
it we are obliged, as we were in Chekhov's earlier ver-
sions, to perceive the man's wretchedness for ourselves
through his efforts to conceal it.

I have also made some slight changes to *Swan Song*. In
the original the old actor performs not only extracts from
Shakespeare, as here, but also a speech from *Boris Go-
dunov* and some lines from another work of Pushkin's,
his great epic poem *Poltava*. The play goes on to end with
Chatsky's bitter farewell to Moscow at the end of Griboyedov's *Woe from Wit*. Once again the play was subject to rewriting, and in earlier editions ended with all or
part of the *Othello* quotation; while in the original story
from which the play was taken the old actor is led miser-
ably off to his dressing-room at the end without ever
demonstrating his vanished greatness at all. I have re-
verted to the *Othello* ending, and also cut the scene from
Hamlet which preceded it. The two extracts from *Lear*
and *Othello* seem a perfectly adequate demonstration of
Svetlovidov's past glories, and while the Pushkin and the
Griboyedov would be as familiar to Russians as the
Shakespeare is to us I can see no way of making them
even recognisable to an English audience. Chekhov
plainly felt that the Shakespeare (in translation) would
present no difficulty to Russians. Whether this disparity

is a testimony to the universality of English drama or to the parochialism of English audiences I do not know.

I have also taken an even greater liberty. The four plays of Chekhov's own in this collection are not quite enough to make an evening by themselves, and I have included a further four which I have adapted myself. They all come (like his own adaptations) from short stories that he wrote in the eighties. *Drama* is based on an original with the same title written in 1887, at the time of *Ivanov.* (It was another great favourite of Tolstoy's; he told people the story of it over and over again and always made himself laugh.) *The Alien Corn* is taken from *In a Foreign Land*, written in 1885; *The Inspector-General* from *An Awl in a Sack* of the same year (the title refers to a Russian saying, 'You can't hide an awl in a sack'); and *The Sneeze* from *The Death of a Government Official* of 1883 (which, according to Chekhov's sister Masha, was based on an incident that actually happened at the Bolshoi). I have included as an appendix a fifth adaptation, *Plots*, taken from a story with the same title written in 1887, which was dropped from the original production of *The Sneeze* for reasons of length, but which might possibly suit another company better than one of the other plays. The stories all first appeared in the humorous journal *Oskolki* (Splinters), under the signature he used as a humorist, 'Antosha Chekhonte'. I have also included in this text the framework that Ronald Eyre, who directed the original production at the Aldwych, devised with my collaboration to link the various items together into a producible whole.

I recognise my presumption in adding to the world's stock of Chekhov plays, but if these adaptations intrigue a few theatregoers into reading the originals, and exploring for themselves the ever more wonderful stories that Chekhov was writing in those amazing years, then my effrontery will be more than justified.

Michael Frayn, 1988

The Sneeze was first presented by Michael Codron at the Theatre Royal, Newcastle-upon-Tyne, on 23 August 1988, and subsequently at the Aldwych Theatre, London, with Rowan Atkinson, Cheryl Campbell, Anthony Dunston, Michael Godley, Olga Lowe, Tricia Morrish, and Timothy West. It was directed by Ronald Eyre and designed by Mark Thompson, with music composed and arranged by Jeremy Sams, and played by Michael Haslam.

Characters

Drama

PAVEL VASILYEVICH, *a writer*
MURASHKINA, *a lady with literary ambitions*
LUKA, *a manservant*

The Alien Corn

KAMYSHEV, *a landowner*
CHAMPUGNE, *his former French tutor*
MISHA, *a footman*

The Sneeze

BRIZZHALOV, *a very senior Government official*
HIS WIFE
CHERVYAKOV, *a very minor Government official*
HIS WIFE

The Bear

POPOVA, *a widow*
SMIRNOV, *a landowner*
LUKA, *an elderly footman*

The Evils of Tobacco

NYUKHIN, *his wife's husband; she being the proprietress of a conservatory of music and a boarding-school for young ladies*

The Inspector-General

A TRAVELLER
A CART DRIVER

19

Swan Song

SVETLOVIDOV, *an actor*
NIKITA IVANICH, *a prompter*

The Proposal

CHUBUKOV, *a landowner*
NATALYA STEPANOVNA, *his daughter*
LOMOV, *a neighbour*

Act One

Opening

Enter the member of the cast who is to be the STORY-
TELLER in Drama.

STORYTELLER. Lord Nelson was sick every time he
went to sea . . . Columbus was trying to get to
India . . . Stalin was training to be a priest . . . And
Chekhov didn't like plays. Or so he once confided to a
fellow-writer.

(*Enter the member of the cast who is to play PAVEL*
VASILYEVICH in Drama.)

PAVEL VASILYEVICH. Except short ones.
STORYTELLER. *The Sneeze*, and other episodes. Four
short plays, and four short stories, by Anton Chekhov.
Number one — Drama . . .

Drama

PAVEL VASILYEVICH, a well-known writer, is sitting
reading a newspaper. The STORYTELLER opens a
volume of Chekhov.

STORYTELLER. (*reads*) Pavel Vasilyevich, the well-
known writer, was sitting one morning hard at work,
when in came his servant Luka . . .

(*Enter LUKA.*)

21

LUKA. Pavel Vasilich!

STORYTELLER. Said Luka to his master.

LUKA. She's here again, sir. A whole hour she's been waiting.

PAVEL VASILYEVICH. (*absorbed in the paper*) What?

LUKA. The lady with the spectacles. She's here again.

PAVEL VASILYEVICH. (*vaguely*) Tell her I'm busy.

LUKA. It's the fifth day in a row, sir.

STORYTELLER. Said Luka.

LUKA. She says it's very urgent. Almost in tears, she is, sir.

PAVEL   VASILYEVICH.   (*vaguely*)   Oh . . . Right . . .

LUKA. Oh, Lord bless you, sir. She'll be so pleased. I'll show her into the study.

(*Exeunt, separately, LUKA and the STORYTELLER. Enter a study. PAVEL VASILYEVICH sits down at the desk, still absorbed in his newspaper.*)

LUKA. (*calling, off*) This way, ma'am! In here!

PAVEL VASILYEVICH. (*appalled*) What?

(*Enter MURASHKINA. She is stout, red-faced, bespectacled, and elaborately dressed. She sweeps in, her hands pressed together in supplication.*)

MURASHKINA. Such an admirer! Every book, every play! Such a talent! Such a pleasure! Murashkina . . . You don't remember — why should you? — we met at the Tarakanovs. No, every word you write! And don't think I'm trying to flatter you — I know how you writers hate flattery — in fact I'm a writer myself — well, I hardly dare say a writer, but yes, I have brought my small drop of honey to the hive—three children's stories—and my late brother had connections with publishing.

PAVEL VASILYEVICH. Ah. Anyway . . .

MURASHKINA. The point being that I hold you in such enormous respect I want to ask your advice. I have lately been brought to bed of a bouncing baby play—if I may put it like that!—and before I let anyone else see it I should like *your* opinion of it.

PAVEL VASILYEVICH. Yes, well, why don't you just put it in the post and . . . ?

MURASHKINA. (*producing a bulky manuscript*) Here!

(*PAVEL VASILYEVICH leaps back in alarm.*)

PAVEL VASILYEVICH. Ah. In that case, leave it with me, and as soon as I have a moment . . .

MURASHKINA. Pavel Vasilyevich! I know how busy you are.

PAVEL VASILYEVICH. I am a little . . .

MURASHKINA. I know every moment is precious to you.

PAVEL VASILYEVICH. Well, I do have a number of . . .

MURASHKINA. I know this is the grossest impertinence. I know you're cursing me in your heart.

PAVEL VASILYEVICH. (*toys with the paperknife*) No, no . . . No, no . . .

MURASHKINA. An hour or two of your time, that's all I'm asking . . .

PAVEL VASILYEVICH. (*holds out his hands for the manuscript*) Yes, yes, I look forward to reading it . . .

MURASHKINA. (*snatches the manuscript back*) I shouldn't dream of putting you to the trouble . . .

PAVEL VASILYEVICH. Oh. Well . . .
MURASHKINA. I'm going to read it to you myself!

(*PAVEL VASILYEVICH starts hurriedly in the direction of the door.*)

PAVEL VASILYEVICH. I have a train to catch.

(*MURASHKINA stops him.*)

MURASHKINA. I implore you! Show me the greatness of your soul!
PAVEL VASILYEVICH. Very well, very well. Five minutes, then.
MURASHKINA. (*getting to her feet*) An hour, no more.
PAVEL VASILYEVICH. Five minutes.
MURASHKINA. Two hours at the outside. (*Quickly starting to read.*) 'Act One, Scene One.' *PAVEL VASILYEVICH sits down at his desk again as she reads, gazing at her as if hanging upon every word.*) 'The luxuriously appointed drawing-room of a country house on the estate of Baron Bogatov. Dasha, the chamber-maid, is dusting the escritoire. Enter Sasha, the footman.
Sasha: Oh, there you are, Dasha!
Dasha: Oh, it's you, Sasha!
Sasha: Dasha . . .
Dasha: Yes, Sasha . . . ?'
I'm establishing their names, you see.

(*PAVEL VASILYEVICH nods.*)

'Sasha: You know what they're saying in the kitchen, Dasha. They're saying as how Anna Sergeyevna Bogatova, the Baron's daughter, who's 19 now, and as lovely as a peach, has taken it into her head to build a school and a hospital on the estate for the likes of us. Whatever is the world coming to?

Dasha: Yes, but her mother don't hold with such goings-on! She believes the likes of us ought to remain in ignorance! They say as how she wants to marry Anna Sergeyevna off to some rich gentleman! I don't know . . . !'

Sasha and Dasha are comic characters, of course. But they are also there to make a serious point, as you'll hear.

(*PAVEL VASILYEVICH nods.*)

'Sasha (*seriously*): Such ructions! And yet how shall we ever see the light without education? How shall we ever learn to appreciate books and plays and such? How shall we ever overcome the terrible darkness in which the Russian people have lived for so many centuries . . . ?'

(*MURASHKINA continues with her reading, but by this time her voice has gradually faded to inaudibility, and been gradually replaced by PAVEL VASILYEVICH's voice.*)

PAVEL VASILYEVICH. (*to himself*) Why me? Why me? Why me? Why me?! *You* write the play—and *I'm* the one who's punished for it! (*MURASHKINA acts an exit.*) No, all right—she's going . . . Hold on—she's coming back . . . (*MURASHKINA acts an entrance.*) She's making an entrance. She's gone all noble. This is the young mistress, is it? Nineteen? Lovely as a peach? As long as she doesn't meet some local intellectual.

MURASHKINA. (*audible again*). '. . . I haven't slept all night. I've been thinking about Valentin Ivanovich, the 22-year-old student who arrived last week.'

PAVEL VASILYEVICH. I knew it! I knew it!

MURASHKINA. 'He's such a strange man! He has enlightened views on popular education—and yet he doesn't believe in friendship or love—he has no real purpose in life! It's up to me to save him . . .' (*MURASHKINA continues inaudibly.*)

PAVEL VASILYEVICH. (*to himself*) She's going to fall in love with him. He's not going to fall in love with her. She's going to renounce him. He's going to be carried off in a cholera epidemic. She's going to devote her life to saving stray pigs . . .

MURASHKINA. You don't think the monologue is a shade long?

PAVEL VASILYEVICH. Monologue! I'm sorry—was I talking to myself? Oh, *your* monologue. No, no! Perfect! Just right!

MURASHKINA. Please don't hesitate to stop me at any point if you have some observation to make. 'Enter Valentin Ivanovich . . .'

PAVEL VASILYEVICH. Stop!

MURASHKINA. Yes?

PAVEL VASILYEVICH. This is not in any way a criticism, but I do have to leave for the country tomorrow morning, so perhaps . . .

MURASHKINA. We must press on, then. 'Enter Valentin Ivanovich . . .' (*She continues inaudibly.*)

PAVEL VASILYEVICH. (*to himself*) So perhaps he could fall into a disused mineshaft before he opens his mouth . . . No?

MURASHKINA. 'Valentin Ivanovich: I have come to talk to you about various matters of public hygiene . . .'

PAVEL VASILYEVICH. No. Never stop them now.

MURASHKINA. 'Anna Sergeyevna: You try to live by the intellect alone! You won't listen to your heart!'

PAVEL VASILYEVICH. Here they go.

MURASHKINA. 'Valentin Ivanovich: The heart?'

PAVEL VASILYEVICH. What is the heart?

MURASHKINA. 'What is the heart?'

PAVEL VASILYEVICH. Something in a textbook on anatomy.

MURASHKINA. 'Something in a textbook on anatomy! If you're using it as the conventional term for what are called feelings, then I don't acknowledge it. Anna Sergeyevna (*shyly*): . . .'

PAVEL VASILYEVICH. How about love?

MURASHKINA. 'How about love?' (*PAVEL VASILYEVICH nods wearily and begins to fall asleep.*) 'Is that just an association of ideas? Tell me frankly — Have you ever loved?

Valentin (*bitterly*): Please — you are touching upon old but still unhealed wounds.

Anna Sergeyevna: What are you thinking about? (*Pause.*)' (*She pauses. PAVEL VASILYEVICH abruptly wakes up.*)

PAVEL VASILYEVICH. (*to himself*) What? What's happened? She's stopped!

MURASHKINA. 'I believe you are unhappy.'

PAVEL VASILYEVICH. (*to MURASHKINA*) No, no! Not at all! Happy as a fish in a frying-pan!

MURASHKINA. (*puzzled*) You believe he's *happy*?

PAVEL VASILYEVICH. *He's* happy? *Who's* happy?

MURASHKINA. Ah. You believe *she* believes he's happy!

PAVEL VASILYEVICH. (*baffled*) Ah.

MURASHKINA. (*thinks about this for a moment, looking at her manuscript*) No. Please feel free to suggest any changes you like. But on this point I must insist. 'I believe you are unhappy. (*She goes to him.*) . . . ?'

(*She continues inaudibly.*)

PAVEL VASILYEVICH. (*to himself*) How long was I asleep for? An hour? Two hours? We must be very near the end. (*MURASHKINA kneels and casts her eyes up to heaven.*) Yes, yes, it's the renunciation scene. We're nearly there. What's she saying?

MURASHKINA. 'Curtain.' (*He gets to his feet, applauding.*) What can I say? Rarely can a curtain have afforded such exquisite pleasure . . .

MURASHKINA. 'Act Two.'

PAVEL VASILYEVICH. Act Two? (*He sinks slowly back into his chair, stunned.*) 'The village street. On stage right is a school, on stage left a hospital. On the steps of the latter sit a crowd of some forty or fifty peasants . . .'

PAVEL VASILYEVICH. (*rising again*) I'm sorry. How many altogether?

MURASHKINA.   Forty   or   fifty.   'In   the background . . .'

PAVEL VASILYEVICH. Forty or fifty acts?

MURASHKINA. Forty or fifty peasants. 'In the background more peasants can be seen taking their belongings to exchange for drink in the tavern . . .'

PAVEL VASILYEVICH. Acts, acts. How many acts?

MURASHKINA. Five. 'From the windows of the school Valentin Ivanovich stands watching . . .' (*She continues inaudibly.*)

PAVEL VASILYEVICH. (*to himself, as he subsides slowly into his chair*) Five. All right. Say the first act took an hour and a half. Five times one is five, plus five times a half, less Act One, that's one and a half, plus say half-an-hour for intervals . . . Might still get away for the weekend . . .

MURASHKINA. 'Suddenly there is a thundering of

hooves. A squadron of Cossacks gallops on stage left . . .'

PAVEL VASILYEVICH. Nothing penny-pinching about this production. What's she going to do with a squadron of Cossacks?

MURASHKINA. '. . . and gallops off again stage right.'

PAVEL VASILYEVICH. Not a lot. (*His eyes begin to close.*) Must keep my eyes open . . . Might be a herd of elephants coming next . . . Shut my eyes for a moment, perhaps . . . Just listen . . .

MURASHKINA. 'Zorza Zorzeva: Zorzn zorzil zoozi zeezn, zeezn zeezn zoozi zorzil.'

PAVEL VASILYEVICH. (*to himself*) That's good. Like that bit.

MURASHKINA. Zarzil Zarzevich: Zoozl! Zoozl! Zoozi zoozn zoozl!

PAVEL VASILYEVICH. (*snores*) Khhhh . . .

MURASHKINA. I beg your pardon?

PAVEL VASILYEVICH. (*hurriedly waking up*) Did I speak?

MURASHKINA. You said 'Khhhh . . .'

PAVEL VASILYEVICH. Exactly. Khhhhamazing! Khhhhwonderful!

MURASHKINA. Thank you. But we've hardly started yet! 'Valentin Ivanovich: No, no, let me go away from here!

Anna Sergeyevna (*frightened*): Why? Why?

Valentin Ivanovich (*aside*): She's gone pale! (To Anna Sergeyevna.) Don't force me to reveal my reasons . . .' (*She continues inaudibly.*)

PAVEL VASILYEVICH. (*to himself*) It's never going to end, is it. I'll never see my wife and children again! Never see another summer! Never hear the birds or smell the flowers!

MURASHKINA. 'Valentin Ivanovich (*Embracing Anna Sergeyevna*): You have raised me from the dead! You have given me new life, as the spring rain gives new life to the waking earth . . .' (*She continues inaudibly.*)

PAVEL VASILYEVICH. (*to himself*) Help! Get me out of here! I demand to see my lawyer! A doctor, quick — get me a doctor! All right, where's the confession? I'll sign, I'll sign!

MURASHKINA. 'Anna Sergeyevna: I love him, Father! I love him more than life itself!
Baron Bogatov: No! No! Kill me if you must, but not that!'

PAVEL VASILYEVICH. (*to himself*) What's she saying?

MURASHKINA. 'Valentin Ivanovich: Kill me, rather! Anna Sergeyevna: No, no — kill me first! Valentin Ivanovich: Kill me! Kill me!'

PAVEL VASILYEVICH. (*to himself*) Oh. Right. Good idea. (*He picks up the paperknife from his desk. As in a dream he creeps up on her from behind.*)

MURASHKINA. (*unaware*) 'Curtain. Act Three. The banks of a great river at sunset. A fleet of barges moves slowly downstream. Surveying this peaceful scene is Anna Sergeyevna.
Anna Sergeyevna: If only we could know where life is leading! What its end, and what its point . . .'

(*PAVEL VASILYEVICH stabs her. She dies. Police whistles. Pandemonium. Enter OMNES. They seize him. PAVEL VASILYEVICH, his composure entirely restored, nonchalantly twists the knife in his pocket handkerchief to clean it.*)

PAVEL VASILYEVICH. Nice twist at the end, though.

(*Blackout.*)

The Alien Corn

Enter a dining-room. The actress who played MUR-ASHKINA in Drama *rises from the dead and becomes the STORYTELLER. She opens a volume of Chekhov's stories and reads aloud while KAMYSHEV and CHAMPUGNE take their places at the dining table.*

STORYTELLER. Second story—*The Alien Corn*. (*Reads.*) A dull Sunday on a country estate. Kamyshev, the owner of the estate, is making a leisurely lunch. Sharing the meal is an elderly Frenchman, Monsieur Champugne, who was once the tutor to Kamyshev's children. But they've all grown up and left home, long ago . . .

(*Exit the STORYTELLER. The full lights come up on the dining table to reveal KAMYSHEV eating and weeping, while CHAMPUGNE waits politely in front of his empty plate. They are being waited on by MISHA, a young footman who is as dull and serviceable as the table. There is a long silence while KAMYSHEV wipes his eyes and blows his nose. At last he is able to speak.*)

KAMYSHEV. Damnation, but that mustard's hot! Down your throat, up your nose, can't speak, can't see. Feel it in every joint. (*MISHA clears the plates and serves the next course.*) That's Russian mustard for you. Wouldn't get the same effect out of your precious French mustard if you swallowed a pot of it.

CHAMPUGNE. (*diplomatically*) Some people like French mustard, some people like Russian.

KAMYSHEV. No one likes French mustard except the

31

French. Put anything in front of a Frenchman, so long as it's French, and he'll eat it. Frogs, rats, cockroaches. You don't like this ham, do you? Of course not — it's Russian. Put a plateful of broken glass in front of you and tell you it's French cooking — you'd scoff it down and ask for more. I know what you French think — if it's Russian it's no good.

CHAMPUGNE. I have never said that.

KAMYSHEV. Anything Russian — terrible. Anything French — *oh, c'est tres joli!* You want to know what I think of France? A handful of dirt. I mean, let's be frank — it's about half the size of my estate! You can go round the whole of France in one day! Step outside the gate in this country and you can keep going forever.

CHAMPUGNE. Certainly, monsieur — Russia is a vast country.

KAMYSHEV. You think the French are the flower of civilisation! Got manners, your Frenchman, I grant you that. Fetches the ladies a chair fast enough, doesn't spit on the floor. But there's no spirit in him! I read somewhere that what you people have is acquired intelligence, all out of books, whereas what we have is natural intelligence. If Russians were taught science properly they'd be the equal of any professor in the world.

CHAMPUGNE. (*politely*) It's possible.

KAMYSHEV. It's not possible — it's so! 'Possible . . .' I don't know what *you've* got to complain about.

CHAMPUGNE. Nothing at all, monsieur.

KAMYSHEV. Thirty years you've been tutor here. Long enough for you, I hope?

CHAMPUGNE. Monsieur.

KAMYSHEV. Always been treated like one of the family, haven't you?

CHAMPUGNE. I have no complaints, monsieur!

KAMYSHEV. I should think not. Always sat here at the family table . . . 'Possible . . .'! No, the Russian mind, I say . . . (*to MISHA:*) Wake up! Next course! (*to CHAMPUGNE:*) . . . The Russian mind is an inventive mind. The only thing we don't know how to do is boast about it. Your Frenchman invents some piece of nonsense and shouts it from the rooftops. Your Russian invents some amazing new thing and gives it to the children to play with. The coachman invented something only the other day. Little man carved out of wood. Pull a string and it does something indecent. He doesn't go around boasting about it . . .! 'Possible', indeed! Tutor? You don't even have to tutor! There's no one left to tutor! They've all grown up and gone! What do you have to do? Get up, get dressed, sprinkle scent on yourself, and come in to lunch. I find your behaviour a little surprising in the circumstances.

CHAMPUGNE. My behaviour?

KAMYSHEV. Complaining about this country . . .

CHAMPUGNE. I haven't complained, monsieur!

KAMYSHEV. There you are! Contradicting again! No, I can't stand the French. Not referring to you, of course . . . Complain about other people—but what about *them*? No morals between the lot of them! If a Russian gets married then he sticks to his wife, and no nonsense about it. God knows what happens in your country. The husband goes off and sits in the café all day—the wife lets in a whole houseful of Frenchmen and dances the can-can with them.

CHAMPUGNE. (*suddenly flaring up, and jumping to his feet*) That is a lie! For the hundredth time, French ladies do not dance the can-can!

KAMYSHEV. Oh, come on—let's not be blinded by prejudice. If the French behave like swine then let's admit it—they behave like swine. We should be grateful to the Germans for beating them.

CHAMPUGNE. (*agitatedly crumpling and uncrumpling his napkin*) If you hate the French so much, monsieur, why do you keep me here?

KAMYSHEV. What else can I do with you?

CHAMPUGNE. (*flings down his napkin dramatically*) Monsieur, I have sat here and listened to your insults for thirty years. But there comes a day when one can listen no longer!

KAMYSHEV. Where are you off to?

CHAMPUGNE. Back to France!

(*Exit CHAMPUGNE. KAMYSHEV continues with his lunch.*)

KAMYSHEV. (*to himself*) Funny. Didn't even wait for the main course. Sad world if you can't pull a leg or two over lunch. (*Silence.*) (*To MISHA.*) I said, not much fun in life if people can't take a joke.

MISHA. No, sir.

KAMYSHEV. You wouldn't fly up, would you, if I teased you about the mustard?

MISHA. No, sir. (*Silence. KAMYSHEV eats.*) KAMYSHEV. Though I don't suppose you've ever tried French mustard.

MISHA. No, sir. (*Silence.*) KAMYSHEV. Or Russian mustard.

MISHA. No, sir.

KAMYSHEV. Not much fun talking to *you*, then, is it?

MISHA. No, sir.

KAMYSHEV. 'No, sir. No, sir . . .' (*to himself.*) What a life. Not careful you end up talking to yourself.

(*Enter CHAMPUGNE, upset and on his dignity, with an armful of underclothes and braces. Ignoring KAMYSHEV and MISHA, he hurries across to the sideboard and begins to hunt through the drawers. KAMYSHEV eats and watches him out of the corner of his eye.*)

KAMYSHEV. Passport?

CHAMPUGNE. Where is it?

KAMYSHEV. Yes, you won't get very far without a passport in this country. One look at you and they'll say, 'Who's this, then?' — 'Monsieur Alphonse Champugne.' 'Where's your passport, then, Monsieur Alphonse Champugne . . . ? What, *no* passport? Perhaps you'd like to take a trip in the opposite direction, then — to Siberia.'

CHAMPUGNE. (*horrified*) Siberia?

KAMYSHEV. You won't find French mustard in Siberia.

CHAMPUGNE. But *you* have my passport! I gave *you* my passport!

KAMYSHEV. Of course. And I put it in a safe place.

CHAMPUGNE. So where is it, then, please?

KAMYSHEV. My dear chap — how should *I* know? That was thirty years ago!

(*CHAMPUGNE gazes at KAMYSHEV in horror. The underclothes and braces begin to slip out of his arms.*)

CHAMPUGNE. Oh, my God, my God! I curse the day I took it into my head to leave my homeland!

KAMYSHEV. You can show the Siberians how to dance the can-can.

CHAMPUGNE. (*weeps*) You've mocking me! You're making sport of me!

KAMYSHEV. (*suddenly laughs*) Of course I am! (*He gets to his feet and advances upon CHAMPUGNE, his arms open.*) My dear, dear fellow! You must learn to take a joke! (*He embraces CHAMPUGNE.*) What a strange chap you are! Can't say a word to you! Fly up like a wildcat!

CHAMPUGNE. (*moved*) *Oh, mon cher monsieur!* But you know I'm devoted to Russia! I'm devoted to you and your children! To leave here would be as hard as to die! But every word you say — it cuts me to the heart!

KAMYSHEV. What a funny fellow, though! Fancy taking offence just because I say a few rude things about the French, of all people! Come on — let's sit down and have our pie. Misha . . . (*KAMYSHEV coaxes CHAMPUGNE back to his place at the table, and MISHA serves the pie.*) Good heavens, Misha here doesn't take offence if I tease him a little! (*He tweaks MISHA's ear. MISHA gives a small cry of pain.*) Do you, Misha?

MISHA. No, sir.

KAMYSHEV. 'No, sir.' You see? (*Unseen by CHAMPUGNE, KAMYSHEV coats the food on CHAMPUGNE's plate with a thick coating of Russian mustard.*) That little Jew of mine who leases the tavern — I call him all kinds of names! Snort like a pig at him! Pull his sidecurls! He doesn't mind a bit! Eat up, then! Friends?

CHAMPUGNE. Friends, friends . . . (*They sit down at the table. CHAMPUGNE takes a mouthful of food.*)

KAMYSHEV. Yes, a Russian knows how to laugh and

enjoy himself. (*CHAMPUGNE abruptly stops eating.*)
Whereas your average Frenchman tends to sit there
looking   as   if   he's   got   a   mouthful   of
mustard . . . (*CHAMPUGNE starts to weep, like KA-
MYSHEV at the beginning.*)

(Blackout.)

The Sneeze

Enter a theatre audience, and various members of the cast, who act as STORYTELLERS.

STORYTELLER 1. *The Sneeze.* One fine evening a Government official, no less fine than the evening itself, was at the theatre. (*Enter BRIZZHALOV, a very senior Government official, accompanied by his WIFE. He hands his hat to the STORYTELLERS, and is ushered to his seat.* He was a very senior Government official . . .

STORYTELLER 2. . . . And with him was his wife.

STORYTELLER 1. They had good seats in the stalls . . .

STORYTELLER 2. And they were having a very enjoyable evening . . .

STORYTELLER 3. And just behind the very important Government official and his wife were sitting a very minor Government official and his wife . . .

(*Enter CHERVYAKOV, a very minor Government official, and his WIFE. They sit in the cheaper seats immediately above and behind the BRIZZHALOVS, very overawed by their surroundings.*)

STORYTELLER 4. Also having a very enjoyable evening.

STORYTELLER 1. When suddenly . . .

(*CHERVYAKOV is seized by the beginnings of a sneeze.*)

STORYTELLER 2. 'When suddenly . . .' Ah, how
often you come across those two words in stories!

STORYTELLER 1. Authors are right, though—life is
full of suddenness!

(*But CHERVYAKOV's sneeze fails to mature. Exeunt
the STORYTELLERS, as the lights change and the
music starts. Both couples settle down to watch the
ballet taking place in front of them.*

*Suddenly CHERVYAKOV is overtaken by an enormous
sneeze. BRIZZHALOV and the others glance briefly
in his direction, but pay no further attention. CHER-
VYAKOV makes a face to his WIFE to demonstrate
humorous embarrassment at having disturbed people, then gets out his handkerchief and blows his nose
extensively. He finds various traces of the sneeze on
his person, and wipes them away with the handkerchief. He is just putting the handkerchief away and
settling down to enjoy the show again when he realises that BRIZZHALOV is cautiously feeling the
bald patch on the back of his head, then inspecting
his fingers, and looking up as if to check whether it is
raining.*

*CHERVYAKOV is greatly dismayed at this. He looks at
MRS CHERVYAKOV, who looks back at him no
less dismayed. He gets his handkerchief out again,
leans over the rail of the gallery, and mops at
BRIZZHALOV's head. BRIZZHALOV looks
round, startled. CHERVYAKOV recognises him, together with his seniority. He jumps to his feet and
starts bowing and bobbing, and demonstrating that
he was wiping BRIZZHALOV's head with his
handkerchief, and trying to introduce his WIFE. The*

THEATREGOERS behind CHERVYAKOV urge him to sit down. BRIZZHALOV nods briefly, dismisses the whole incident, and turns back to watch the show.

But now CHERVYAKOV's peace of mind has been destroyed. He tries to explain to his wife, by pointing to BRIZZHALOV's epaulettes, then bowing at his back, and miming various possible forms of execution, how important BRIZZHALOV is. BRIZZHALOV looks around, frowning, disturbed by the whispering. CHERVYAKOV bobs up, smiling and demonstrating elaborate deference. The THEATREGOERS behind make him sit down.

When BRIZZHALOV has turned to face the front again, CHERVYAKOV begins to worry about whether he has cleared up all the traces that his sneeze left upon BRIZZHALOV. He takes the opera-glasses from his wife and inspects BRIZZHALOV through them. He finds what he is looking for, nerves himself, boldly and firmly wipes BRIZZHALOV's head, then quickly looks at the stage through his opera-glasses. But BRIZZHALOV swings round immediately, now considerably irritated. CHERVYAKOV tries to gesture that he has now successfully completed the clean-up operation, and puts his handkerchief away in his pocket. BRIZZHALOV turns back to look at the show again. The CHERVYAKOVS watch in horror as the BRIZZHALOVS exchange whispered comments, and MRS BRIZZHALOV turns round briefly to look at this tiresome couple behind.

The CHERVYAKOVS try to re-immerse themselves in the ballet. But an appalling thought has now struck MRS CHERVYAKOV. She looks at her husband with a hand to her mouth. He silently begs her to tell him what is worrying her. She indicates BRIZZHALOV; CHERVYAKOV nods impatiently. She indicates CHERVYAKOV; he nods impatiently again. Then she mimes spitting at BRIZZHALOV, and puts her hand back to her mouth in horror. CHERVYAKOV does not understand. He repeats the sequence interrogatively. He points at BRIZZHALOV; his wife nods. He points at himself; his wife nods. He mimes spitting. She nods again. Suddenly the kopeck drops. CHERVYAKOV puts his hand to his mouth in horror as well. He leans down and taps BRIZZHALOV on the shoulder. BRIZZHALOV looks round wearily. CHERVYAKOV shakes his head and waves his finger, desperately trying to assure BRIZZHALOV that he has misunderstood. But BRIZZHALOV can't understand what it is that he has misunderstood. CHERVYAKOV mimes spitting at him to explain. BRIZZHALOV starts back in amazement, wiping his face. CHERVYAKOV signals wildly desperate negatives, then beckons BRIZZHALOV towards him and mimes sneezing over him instead. BRIZZHALOV starts back again, and gets out his handkerchief to clean himself up.

(*CHERVYAKOV bobs, dabs at BRIZZHALOV, clutches at his head in helpless agony, until the BRIZZHALOVS eventually calm down again and return their attention to the show. MRS CHERVYAKOV mimes a light laugh to her husband, then reverts to appalled anxiety. CHERVYAKOV doesn't understand. He mimes the light laugh interrogatively back to her. She points at BRIZZHALOV and then at him, and mimes the light laugh again. He takes the point. He rehearses the light laugh once or twice, then leans forward, trying hopelessly to catch BRIZZHALOV's eye from behind to demonstrate his light laugh. He looks at his wife; it won't work. She produces a pencil from her reticule, passes it to her husband together with the programme, and urges him to write. With shaking hands he scribbles something down, then leans forward and jiggles the programme nervously about next to BRIZZHALOV's ear. BRIZZHALOV brushes absently at his ear. CHERVYAKOV looks at his wife; what now? She demonstrates putting the programme where BRIZZHALOV can see it. CHERVYAKOV leans further out and dangles the programme in front of BRIZZHALOV's face.*

For a moment BRIZZHALOV just sits there, with the programme obscuring his view of the stage. Then he snatches it out of CHERVYAKOV's hands and jumps up to confront him. The CHERVYAKOVS both demonstrate their light laugh. BRIZZHALOV stares at them incredulously, and draws his wife's attention to the fact that they are now being openly mocked. Then he beckons to CHERVYAKOV, who stops laughing and leans eagerly forward. BRIZZHALOV reaches up and slaps his face.

The BRIZZHALOVS sit down, all outraged dignity, and focus their attention pointedly upon the show. CHERVYAKOV feels his cheek, in a state of shock, then clutches at his heart. His eyes open very wide. He stands up, scarcely able to keep his balance, and makes desperate efforts to climb over his neighbours and leave, while MRS CHERVYAKOV shouts silently for help.

The music ends, and the BRIZZHALOVS start to applaud. CHERVYAKOV staggers about, holding his heart. The BRIZZHALOVS look round at the commotion behind them. MRS CHERVYAKOV hurriedly abandons her efforts to help her husband and starts to applaud as well. She draws CHERVYAKOV's attention to the fact that the BRIZZHALOVS are watching, and even CHERVYAKOV himself makes efforts to applaud and smile and behave deferentially as he sinks dying to his knees, and falls bodily forward into BRIZZHALOV's lap.

Curtain.

The Bear

Enter the rest of the cast, as servants, to set the stage for
    The Bear.

ONE OF THE CAST. (*announces*) *The Bear.*

(*The drawing-room in POPOVA's country residence.
    Enter POPOVA, a charming widow with an estate
    and dimples, and LUKA, POPOVA's elderly foot-
    man. POPOVA is in deep mourning, with a photo-
    graph from which she never lifts her eyes.*)

LUKA. It's not right, madam . . . You'll only go and
do yourself a mischief so . . . Cook and parlourmaid
are out picking berries—every breath you draw out
there today is a joy from heaven. Why, even the cat
knows how to take her pleasure in life—her, too, she's
out of doors, catching the little birds. And here you are,
sitting inside the live day long like a nun in a nunnery,
and no pleasure in life at all. Just you think, now, a whole
year's gone by since you set foot outside the house!

POPOVA. Nor shall I set foot outside it ever. Why
should I? My life is over. *He* is lying in his grave, and I
have entombed myself within these four walls. We've
both died.

LUKA. Hark at you! That I should hear such things!
Your husband's dead, and there it is—it was God's will,
and may his soul rest in peace. You've grieved your grief,
and that's enough, it's time to put an end to it. You've
forgotten all your neighbours. You won't go to them,
and you won't let them come to you. Forgive me, but we
live like spiders—we never see the white light of day.
The mice have eaten our livery . . . The district's full of

44

gentlemen. There's a regiment over in town, and the officers — a sugar-plum, every one, a delight to the eye! Looks don't last for ever! Ten years from now you'll be the one wanting to show off your fine feathers to the officers, you'll be the one wanting to throw dust in their eyes, and then it'll be too late.

POPOVA. (*decisively*) Please — never mention the subject again! Since my husband died, as you know, life has lost all meaning for me. I swore on his grave never to come out of mourning and never to look upon the light of day. You understand? Let his shade see how I love him . . . All right, I know it was no secret from you that he treated me badly, that he was cruel to me and even . . . yes, unfaithful to me. But *I* shall be faithful unto the grave — I shall prove to him that *I* am capable of love. And he'll see at last from beyond the tomb exactly what sort of woman I was.

LUKA. Better to take a walk in the garden than say such things, better to have Toby and Giant harnessed up and call on your neighbours.

POPOVA. Oh . . . ! (*Weeps.*)

LUKA. Madam! Sweet madam! What's this, now? Lord have mercy!

POPOVA. He loved Toby so much! He always rode Toby when he was going over to the Korchagins or the Vlasovs. He was such a wonderful horseman! Such a graceful bearing as he hauled with all his might on the reins! Do you remember? Oh, Toby, Toby! See that he's given an extra handful of oats today.

LUKA. Ma'am.

(*An urgent peal on the doorbell.*)

POPOVA. (*starts*) Who's that? Tell them I'm not at home.

LUKA. Very good, ma'am.

(*Exit LUKA.*)

POPOVA. (*looking at the photograph*) You watch, Nikolai — you'll see I'm capable of love and forgiveness. While I have breath in my body, while this poor heart of mine still beats, my love will never die. (*Laughs, on the verge of tears.*) Aren't you ashamed of yourself? Here am I, locking myself away like to nice good little wife and being faithful to you unto the grave, and there are you . . . Well, you should be ashamed of yourself!

(*Enter LUKA.*)

LUKA. (*in alarm*) Madam, it's someone asking for you. He wants to see you . . .
POPOVA. You told him, I presume, that I have been at home to no one since the day my husband died?
LUKA. I did so, but he wouldn't pay no heed. He says it's a very pressing matter.
POPOVA. I — am — not — at home!
LUKA. I told him! But all he does is swear, the great hobgoblin, and comes barging in! He's got into the dining-room!
POPOVA. (*in irritation*) Very well. Show him in, then. Such boorishness! (*Exit LUKA.*) How tedious these people are! What do they want with me? Why must they intrude upon me? (*Sighs.*) No, I see I shall have to retire to a nunnery in good earnest . . . (*Reflects.*) A nunnery, yes, why not?

(*Enter SMIRNOV, a landowner in the prime of life, and LUKA.*)

SMIRNOV. (*to LUKA*) Blockhead! Talk too much, that's your trouble! Jackass! (*Sees POPOVA*) Smirnov. Grigory Stepanovich Smirnov, landowner and lieutenant of artillery, retired. I am obliged to trouble you on a matter of extreme urgency.

POPOVA. (*without offering her hand*) What do you want?

SMIRNOV. Your late husband, with whom I had the honour to be acquainted, left debts outstanding, on two notes of hand in my favour, amounting to twelve hundred rubles. Since the interest on my mortgage falls due tomorrow I should be grateful if you would pay me the money today.

POPOVA. Twelve hundred rubles . . . And how had my husband incurred these debts?

SMIRNOV. He used to buy oats off me.

POPOVA. (*to LUKA, sighing*) Yes, Luka, don't forget to tell them to give Toby an extra handful of oats today. (*Exit LUKA.*) If my husband left debts to you then of course I shall pay them. Forgive me, though—I've no money in hand today. My steward will be back from town the day after tomorrow, and I will tell him to pay you what you're owed, but until then I cannot oblige . . . In addition to which it's exactly seven months today since my husband died, and I am in no mood to concern myself with money matters.

SMIRNOV. If I don't pay the interest tomorrow, however, I'm in a mood to go head over heels into the bankruptcy court! They're going to seize my estate!

POPOVA. You will get your money the day after tomorrow.

SMIRNOV. I don't need it the day after tomorrow—I need it today.

POPOVA. Forgive me, but I can't pay it today.

SMIRNOV. And I can't wait until the day after tomorrow.

POPOVA. But what can I do, if I haven't got it?

SMIRNOV. So you can't pay it, then?

POPOVA. I can't pay it.

SMIRNOV. Ah. And that's your final word?

POPOVA. That's my final word.

SMIRNOV. Positively your final word?

POPOVA. Positively my final word.

SMIRNOV. My most humble thanks. I shan't forget this. (*Shrugs.*) And still they expect me to keep calm about it! I've just met the tax-collector on the way here. 'Grigory Stepanovich', he says, 'why are you always in such a temper?' Well, for pity's sake, how could I not be in a temper? I'm desperate for money. Started out yesterday at the crack of dawn — went round everyone who owes me. Not one of them paid up! Got dog-tired, spent the night next to the vodka barrel in some god-forsaken tavern. Wind up here, forty miles from home, think I'll get my hands on something at last, and I'm greeted with 'not in the mood'! Temper? Of course I'm in a temper!

POPOVA. I made myself quite clear, I think. My steward will be back from town, and then you'll get your money.

SMIRNOV. I haven't come to see your steward; I've come to see you! Why, by all the flaming devils of hell — pardon my language — why should I want to see your steward?

POPOVA. My dear sir, forgive me. I am not accustomed to these curious turns of phrase, nor to being spoken to in that tone of voice. That is as much as I am prepared to listen to.

(*She makes a swift exit.*)

SMIRNOV. How about that? Not in the mood . . . Seven months ago her husband died! What about *me*, though? Have I got to pay my interest or haven't I? All right, your husband's dead, you're not in the mood, and all the rest of it, your steward's gone off somewhere, damn him — and what am *I* supposed to do? Wave my creditors goodbye from an air-balloon? Take a running jump and bash my head against the wall? I go to see Gruzdyov — he's not in. Yaroshevich — he's gone into hiding. I curse Kuritzin halfway to hell and practically throw him out of the window. Mazutov's got cholera, and this one's *not in the mood*. Just you wait, though! You'll find out who you're dealing with! They're not going to make a fool of me, damn them! I'm going to stay here until she pays up! (*Calls.*) Fellow!

(*Enter LUKA.*)

LUKA. Yes, sir?
SMIRNOV. Water! (*Exit LUKA.*) No, but the logic of it! A man's ready to hang himself — and she won't pay up because, oh dear me, she's not inclined to concern herself with money matters! A real piece of feminine logic! That's precisely why I never have liked and never will like talking to women. I'd rather sit on a barrel of gunpowder.

(*Enter LUKA. He serves the water.*)

LUKA. Madam's indisposed. She's not receiving.
SMIRNOV. Get out! (*Exit LUKA.*) Indisposed! Not receiving! All right, my precious — don't receive! I'm going to stay right here until you hand over the money. Be indisposed for a week, if you like — I'll stay here for a

week. Indisposed for a year — I'll stay here for a year. I'm going to have what's mine! You won't soften my heart by being all in black, or having dimples in your cheeks . . . We know all about dimples! (*Calls out of the window.*) Semyon, unharness! We shan't be leaving for some time! I'm staying here! Go to the stables — tell them to give the horses oats! (*Moves away from the window.*) Feel terrible. Intolerable heat, rotten night's sleep, . . . My head's aching . . . Perhaps I should have a glass of vodka? Perhaps I should. (*Calls.*) Fellow!

(*Enter LUKA.*)

LUKA. Yes, sir?
SMIRNOV. A glass of vodka! (*Exit LUKA.*) Agh! (*Sits down and takes a look at himself.*) Must admit I'm a bit of a sight. Covered in dust, mud all over my boots; haven't had a wash or a comb through my hair; straw on my waistcoat . . . Maybe she took me for a bandit. (*Yawns.*) Not very polite, appearing in someone's drawing-room in this state . . . Never mind, though — I'm not here as a guest, I'm here as a creditor, and no one's laid down the correct wear for creditors . . .

(*Enter LUKA. He serves the vodka.*)

LUKA. Very much at home you're making yourself, sir.
SMIRNOV. (*angrily*) What?
LUKA. I never meant . . . I only meant . . .
SMIRNOV. Who do you think you're talking to? Hold your tongue!

(*Enter POPOVA, her eyes downcast.*)

POPOVA. My dear sir, I have long since grown unaccustomed, in my isolation, to the sound of the human voice, and I cannot bear shouting. I earnestly beseech you to end this intrusion!

SMIRNOV. Pay me the money and I'll go.

POPOVA. I've told you quite plainly: I have no money to hand at present — you must wait until the day after tomorrow.

SMIRNOV. I also had the honour to tell you quite plainly: I don't need the money the day after tomorrow — I need it today. If you don't pay me the money today, then tomorrow there will be nothing for it but to hang myself.

POPOVA. But what can I do if I haven't *got* the money? Such an extraordinary way to behave!

SMIRNOV. So you're not going to pay me now? No?

POPOVA. I can't.

SMIRNOV. In that case I shall stay here until I get it. (*Sits down.*) You're going to pay me the day after tomorrow? Fine! Then I shall sit here like this until the day after tomorrow. Stay sat here precisely so . . . (*Jumps up.*) Listen — have I got to pay the interest tomorrow or haven't I?

POPOVA. My dear sir, I must ask you not to shout! We're not in the stables!

SMIRNOV. I'm not talking about stables. I'm simply asking you — Have I got to pay the interest tomorrow or haven't I?

POPOVA. You don't know how to behave in female company!

SMIRNOV. I most certainly do know how to behave in female company!

POPOVA. No, you don't! You're a coarse, ill-brought-up fellow! Decent people don't speak to women so!

SMIRNOV. Oh, but this is amazing! How do you want me to talk to you? In French, perhaps? (*Lisps angrily.*) *Madame, je vous prie* . . . How utterly enchanting that you won't pay the money . . . *Ah, pardon* for troubling you! What utterly enchanting weather today! And black is absolutely your colour! (*Bows and scrapes.*)

POPOVA. That's coarse and not very clever.

SMIRNOV. (*mimics her*) 'Coarse and not very clever.' And I don't know how to behave in female company! Madam, I have seen more women in my time than you've seen sparrows! Three duels I have fought over women! Twelve women I have thrown over — and been thrown over by nine more. Oh, yes! There was a time when I behaved like an idiot, when I was all sweet words and soft music, all scattered pearls and clicking heels . . . I loved, I suffered, I sighed to the moon, I felt weak at the knees, I melted, I went hot and cold . . . I loved passionately, I loved desperately, I loved all the ways there are to love, God help me, I chattered like a magpie about the emancipation of women, I spent half my substance on the tender passion, but now — no, thank you! You won't catch me like that now! I've had enough! Dark, mysterious eyes, scarlet lips, dimples, moonlight, whispers, panting breath — madam, I wouldn't give you a brass kopeck for the lot of it! Women? From the highest to the lowest — present company excepted — they're all hypocrites, fakers, gossip-mongers, grudgebearers, and liars down to their finger-tips; all vain and petty-minded and merciless; and as for what's in here . . . (*He strikes his forehead.*) . . . then forgive me if I'm frank — but a chaffinch could knock spots off any philosopher in a skirt! Look at one of the so-called gentle sex and what do you see? Fine muslins and ethereal essences, a goddess walking the earth, a million delights. But you look into her heart and what is she then? A common or garden crocodile! (*He seizes the back of a chair, which splinters and breaks.*) But the most outrageous thing of all — this crocodile for some reason thinks its crowning achievement, its privilege and monopoly, is the tender passion! Because you can hang me up by my heels, damn it, if a woman knows how to love anything but a lapdog! All a woman can do in love is whimper and snivel! Where a man suffers and sacrifices, all a woman's love consists in is swirling her skirt around and leading him ever more firmly by the nose. You have the misfortune to be a woman, so you know what women are like. Tell me, in all honesty — have you ever in your life seen a woman who could be sincere and constant and true? You haven't!

POPOVA. So who, in your opinion, if I may ask, is constant and true in love? Not a man, by any chance?

SMIRNOV. A man, certainly, a man!

POPOVA. A man! (*Gives an angry laugh.*) A man — constant and true in love! News to me, I must say! (*Heatedly.*) Constant and true — men? If that's what you're telling me then let me inform you that of all the men I have ever known the best was my late husband. I loved him passionately. I loved him with my whole being, as only a young and intelligent woman can love. I gave him my youth and happiness, my life and fortune; I breathed him; I prayed to him like a heathen. And what happened? This best of men deceived me most shamelessly at every step! He left me on my own for weeks at a time — he pursued other women in front of my eyes, he betrayed me, he squandered my money right and left, he mocked my feelings . . . And in spite of it all I loved him and I was true to him . . . And dead as he is, I remain true and constant. I have entombed myself forever within these four walls and I shall wear this mourning unto my grave . . .

SMIRNOV. (*with a scornful laugh*) Mourning! What do you take me for? As if I didn't know why you were wearing this fancy dress, or why you'd shut yourself up inside these four walls! Oh yes! Because it's so mysterious and poetic! Some young mooncalf in cadet-school goes past the estate, some half-pint poet, and he looks up at the windows and he thinks: 'That's where she lives, the mysterious lady who has shut herself up within four walls for love of her husband.' We know all those tricks!

POPOVA. (*flaring up*) What? How dare you say such things to me!

SMIRNOV. You've buried yourself alive, but you haven't forgotten to powder your nose!

POPOVA. How dare you talk to me like this!

SMIRNOV. Don't shout at me, thank you—I'm not your steward! I'll call a spade a spade, if you please. I'm not a woman and I'm accustomed to speaking my mind! So kindly stop your shouting!

POPOVA. I'm not shouting—you're shouting! Kindly go away and leave me alone!

SMIRNOV. Give me the money and I'll go.

POPOVA. I won't give you the money!

SMIRNOV. Oh yes you will!

POPOVA. Not a kopeck, so there! You can just go away and leave me alone!

SMIRNOV. I don't have the pleasure of being your husband or your fiancé, so don't make scenes at me, if you please. (*Sits down.*) I don't like it.

POPOVA. (*choking with anger*) You've sat yourself down?

SMIRNOV. I have.

POPOVA. I've no desire to converse with impertinent

hobbledehoys! Kindly get out of here! (*Pause.*) You won't go?

SMIRNOV. No.

POPOVA. No?

SMIRNOV. No!

POPOVA. Very well, then! (*Rings. (Enter Luka.*) Luka, show this gentleman out!

LUKA. (*goes up to SMIRNOV*) Sir, will you go away when you're told? There's nothing here for you . . .

SMIRNOV. (*jumping up*) Hold your tongue! Who do you think you're talking to? I'll chop you up for salad!

LUKA. (*clutching his heart*) Oh, Lord above! Oh, by all the saints! (*Falls into a chair.*) Oh, I'm going to pass right out! I can't breathe!

POPOVA. Where's Dasha, then? Dasha! (*Calls.*) Dasha! Pelageya! Dasha! (*Rings.*)

LUKA. Oh! They're all out picking berries! There's no one in the house! I'm going to pass clean out! Water!

POPOVA. Kindly get out of here!

SMIRNOV. Would you mend your manners a little?

POPOVA. (*bunching her fists and stamping her feet*) You peasant! You coarse bear! You lout! You monster!

SMIRNOV. I beg your pardon? What did you say?

POPOVA. I said you're a bear, you're a monster!

SMIRNOV. (*advancing on her*) What right do you have, may I ask, to insult me?

POPOVA. Yes, I'm insulting you! What of it? You think I'm frightened of you?

SMIRNOV. And you think you can go round insulting people with impunity, do you, just because you're a woman? I demand satisfaction!

LUKA. Oh, Lord above! Oh, by all the saints! Water!

SMIRNOV. With pistols! I don't give a straw if you're a member of the weaker sex! You want equality?—Then let's have equality, and to hell with it! Just give me satisfaction!

POPOVA. You want to fight a duel? By all means!

SMIRNOV. Here and now!

POPOVA. Here and now! My husband left a pair of pistols. I'll go and get them. (*Hurries towards the door and then returns.*) It will give me the greatest pleasure to put a bullet in your thick wooden head! To hell with you!

(*Exit Popova.*)

SMIRNOV. I'll wing her like a chicken! I'm not some sentimental young puppy! There's no weaker sex as far as I'm concerned!

LUKA. Sweet kind sir . . . ! (*Goes down on his knees.*) Have pity on an old man, and go away from here! You've frightened me to death, and now you're going to start fighting duels!

SMIRNOV. (*paying him no attention*) Fighting duels! Now that really is equality, that really is the emancipation of women! Both sexes level! I'll shoot her on principle! But what sort of woman is she? (*Mimics her.*) 'To hell with you . . . I'll put a bullet in your thick wooden head . . .' What sort of woman is that? She went quite red—her eyes flashed . . . She took up the challenge! Upon my soul, I've never seen such a thing in my life . . .

LUKA. Go away, sir! For the love of God, now!

SMIRNOV. This is something *like* a woman! This is something that makes sense to me! A real woman! Not some whingeing, whining, wishy-washy creature, but fire, gunpowder, skyrockets! Shame to kill her, in fact!

LUKA. (*weeps*) Dear good sir, go away, go away!

SMIRNOV. I've taken a liking to her! A positive liking! Dimples and all! What an astonishing woman!

(*POPOVA enters with the pistols.*)

POPOVA. Here are the pistols. But before we fight, kindly show me how to use them. I've never held a pistol in my life.

LUKA. God save us! I'll go and fetch the gardener and the coachman. What brought this plague down on our heads?

(*Exit LUKA*)

SMIRNOV. (*examining the pistols*) Now, there are various different types of gun in use. There are special Mortimer percussion-lock duelling pistols. But these are revolvers. Smith and Wesson system — double action with extractor, centre fire. Fine guns! Worth at least ninety rubles a pair. Now, you hold a revolver like this . . . (*Aside.*) Her eyes, though, her eyes! She'd start a forest fire with them!

POPOVA. Like that?

SMIRNOV. That's the way . . . Then you cock it . . . Take aim like this . . . Head back a little! Extend the arm properly . . . That's right . . . Then you press your finger on this little thing — and that's all there is to it. Rule number one: don't get excited, and don't rush taking aim. Try to keep your arm steady.

POPOVA. All right . . .

SMIRNOV. Right. (*They stand back to back.*) I must warn you, though — I shall fire into the air.

POPOVA. This really is the limit! Why?

SMIRNOV. Because . . . because . . . That's my business!

POPOVA. What, lost your nerve? Have you? Aha! No, sir, you won't get out of it like that! I shan't rest until I've put a bullet into your head! Into this head here, this loathsome head! So, you've lost your nerve, have you?

SMIRNOV. Yes—lost my nerve.

POPOVA. You're lying! Why don't you want to fight?

SMIRNOV. Because . . . because . . . I've taken a liking to you.

POPOVA. (*with an angry laugh*) He's taken a liking to me! He has the gall to say he's taken a liking to me! (*Stands back to back with him.*) Please.

(*SMIRNOV silently lays down his revolver, takes his cap, and goes. He stops at the door, and for a while they look at each other in silence. Then he goes uncertainly across to her.*)

SMIRNOV. Listen . . . Are you still angry with me? I'm as cross as two sticks myself, but the thing is . . . How can I put it . . . ? Listen, the fact is, not to mince words, this is rather a how-do-you-do . . . (*Shouts.*) I mean, is it my fault if I like you? (*Seizes the back of a chair, which splinters and breaks.*) Very fragile furniture you've got, damn it! I like you! You see? I'm . . . I'm rather in love with you!

POPOVA. Get away from me! I hate you.

SMIRNOV. My God, but what a woman! I've never seen anything like it in my life! I'm finished! I'm done for! Caught like a mouse in a mousetrap.

POPOVA. Get back, or I'll fire!

SMIRNOV. Fire away! You don't know what happiness it would be to die in the sight of those miraculous eyes— to be shot by a revolver held by this tiny soft hand . . . I've gone mad! Decide now, because if I leave we shall never see each other again! I'm a landowner— decent sort—ten thousand a year—fine stable—hit a kopeck in the air—Will you be my wife?

POPOVA. (*brandishing the revolver, outraged*) I demand satisfaction!

SMIRNOV. I've gone completely mad! Don't know what I'm doing . . . (*Shouts.*) Fellow! Water!

POPOVA. (*shouts*) Give me satisfaction!

SMIRNOV. Mad as a hatter! Fallen in love like a schoolboy! (*He seizes her hand. She cries out in pain.*) I love you! (*Kneels.*) I love you as I've never loved before! Twelve women I've thrown over — been thrown over by nine more — but not one of them I loved the way I love you . . . Turned into a heap of jelly . . . Here I am, kneeling like an idiot, offering you my hand . . . Should be ashamed of myself! Haven't fallen in love for five years — swore to high heaven — and now all of a sudden — head over heels like a hunter off a horse! I'm proposing to you. Yes or no? Don't want to? Then don't! (*Gets up and goes quickly across to the door.*)

POPOVA. Wait . . .

SMIRNOV. (*stops*) Well?

POPOVA. Nothing. Go . . . Or rather, wait . . . No — go, go! I hate the sight of you! Or no . . . Don't go! Oh, if you only knew what a rage I'm in, what a tearing rage! (*Throws the revolver down on the table.*) My fingers are all swollen from that horrible thing . . . (*Tears at her handkerchief in her fury.*) What are you standing there for? Get out!

SMIRNOV. Farewell.

POPOVA. Yes, yes — off you go, then! (*Shouts.*) Where are you going? Wait a moment . . . Oh, be off with you! Heavens, I'm in such a rage! Don't come near me, don't come near me!

SMIRNOV. (*going to her*) I'm in a great rage with myself! Fallen in love like a schoolboy, got down on my knees . . . Gone hot and cold all over . . . (*Rudely.*) I love you! That's the last thing I need, to go falling in love with you! I've got the interest to pay, I've got the hay to get in, and now you on top of it all . . . (*Puts his arm around her waist.*) Never forgive myself for this . . .

POPOVA. Get away from me! Take your hands off me! I hate you! I demand satisfaction! (*A prolonged kiss. Enter LUKA holding an axe, the GARDENER with a rake, the COACHMAN with a pitchfork, and VARIOUS WORKMEN with staves.*)

LUKA. (*at the sight of the kissing couple*) Oh, Lord preserve us!

(*Pause.*)

POPOVA. (*with downcast eyes*) Luka, tell them in the stables — no oats for Toby at all today.

Curtain.

Act Two

The Evils of Tobacco

*The platform of an assembly hall in a provincial town.
Enter NYUKHIN, a man who is his wife's husband; she
being the proprietress of a conservatory of music and
a boarding-school for young ladies. He is wearing a
worn and ancient tailcoat. He makes a majestic entrance, bows, and adjusts his waistcoat.*

NYUKHIN. Ladies and, if I may say so, gentlemen.
(*Combs his fingers through his sideboards.*) It has been
suggested to my wife that at this point I should give a talk
on some improving theme. So . . . A talk? All right — a
talk. It's all the same to me. I'm not a professor of anything, of course, I'm not someone with academic qualifi-
cations, but I have none the less worked for the past
thirty years — and worked without cease, worked, I
might add, to the detriment of my health — on various
questions of pure science — turning them over in my
mind, and even on occasion writing learned articles, or
rather not exactly learned articles, but something of the
sort, in the local paper. I recently composed a very substantial article, I might say, under the title 'Certain in-
sects and the damage they do'. My daughters thought
very highly of it, particularly the section on bedbugs, but
then I reread it and tore it up. Because whatever you
write it makes no difference — it all just comes back to
insect powder. We've even got bedbugs in the
piano . . . I have chosen, as the subject of today's talk,
tobacco and the harm it does. (*Takes a snuffbox out of his
pocket and opens it.*) I've no personal feelings in the

matter, but my wife felt it would be a suitable choice, and . . . (*He takes a pinch.*) . . . it makes no odds to me. (*Sneezes.*) But I do suggest, ladies and gentlemen, that you treat what I have to say with all due seriousness . . . (*Sneezes.*) . . . otherwise I might as well save my breath. If anyone here finds lectures on scientific subjects as dry as dust, then, please, let him . . . (*Sneezes, and then looks at the contents of the snuffbox suspiciously.*) I believe my daughters have been putting something in here again . . . Yes, if anyone does, I say, let him stand up now and . . . (*Blows his nose.*) . . . depart forthwith. I would ask any doctors present to pay particular attention. They may pick up a few useful tips, because tobacco, beside its harmful effects, has medical applications as well. Thus, for example, if we place a fly inside a snuffbox, we discover it dies, most probably from nervous disorder. Tobacco, I think I may safely say, is of vegetable origins . . . When I speak in public I tend to wink my right eye, but please attach no significance to this — it's merely a result of nervous tension. I am in fact a martyr to nervous tension, and I started winking my right eye in 1889, on the thirteenth of September of that year, the very day my wife presented me with my fourth daughter. All my daughters have been born on the thirteenth of the month . . . However . . . (*Glances at his watch.*) . . . time is running out and we mustn't let ourselves be distracted from the matter in hand. Let me merely remark that my wife runs a conservatoire of music and a private boarding-academy for young ladies, or not exactly an academy, perhaps, but something of that sort. Strictly between ourselves, my wife is fond of complaining about the world's shortcomings, but she has a little money put by, some forty or fifty thousand rubles, I believe, while I have not a kopeck to my name. Well, there you are. I look after all the housekeeping in the school. I buy the provisions, manage the servants, keep account of the outgoings, stitch the copybooks, get rid of bedbugs, walk my wife's dog, and catch the mice. I make sure there are no more than five girls to a tooth-brush, and no more than ten to a towel . . . Last night I had the task of issuing the cook with flour and fat, be-cause we were going to have pancakes. Well, now, today, to cut a long story short, when the pancakes were already made, my wife arrived in the kitchen to say that three girls were having their pancakes stopped for bad con-duct. So we were three pancakes over. What were we going to do with them? First my wife said to put them away in the cellar, but then she thought for a moment and with great kindness she said: 'You can eat them yourself, dummy.' That's what she calls me when she's not in a good mood — 'dummy'. Or 'snake-in-the-grass'. Or 'Satan'. I don't know why Satan. She's usually not in a good mood. Take yesterday, for instance. She wouldn't give me any dinner. 'What's the point of feeding you?' she says. 'You dummy.' Anyway, the result of all this was that I just gulped the pancakes down without chewing them, which may account for some of the winking now. However . . . (*Looks at his watch.*) . . . We've let ourselves get somewhat carried away. To return to our subject, then . . . Though I'm sure you'd prefer to be istening to some symphony concert, or something out of an opera. (*Sings.*) I've forgotten where that comes from. Speaking of forgetting, I also forgot to mention that apart from all the housekeeping in my wife's school I'm re-sponsible for the teaching of mathematics, physics, chemistry, geography, history, tonic sol-fa, and litera-ture, et cetera. For dancing, singing, and drawing my wife charges extra, though in fact I'm the one who teaches them as well. Our conservatoire is located in Five Dogs Lane, number thirteen. That's probably why I haven't had much success in life, because we live at number thirteen. Also my daughters were all born on the thirteenth, and the house has thirteen windows . . . Anyway . . . My wife is available for consultation at home, no appointment necessary, and the school prospectus can be obtained from the janitor for thirty kopecks. (*Gets some leaflets out of his pocket.*) I could pass these round, for that matter, if anyone's interested. Thirty kopecks! Anyone? (*Pause.*) No one? Twenty kopecks? (*Pause.*) Well, never mind. Yes, number thirteen. Nothing's gone right for me; I've just got older and stupider . . . Here I am giving this talk, and to look at me you'd think I was as merry as a cricket. But inside I feel like screaming at the top of my voice, or taking wing and flying to the other end of the earth. And I've no one to tell my troubles to. You'll say, 'What about your daughters?' What about my daughters? I talk to them and they laugh at me . . . Seven daughters, my wife's got . . . No, just a moment — six . . . No, seven! Twenty-eight, the eldest; seventeen, the youngest. There's only one man in the entire establishment, and that's me. But parents entrusting their daughters to us need have no fears on that score. My wife handles the situation so delicately that the girls don't think of me as a member of the opposite sex at all . . . (*Absently takes out his snuffbox as he talks.*) Yes, my life hasn't been all it might have been, but as a father, as a family man . . . (*Is about to take a pinch of snuff when he stops, looks at it suspiciously, and smells it cautiously.*) Pepper, the little she-devils . . . I hope no one will think my daughters' pranks are any reflection on school discipline. In matters of discipline the school can only work hand in hand with the family. It's the families that I blame in these cases . . . No, thirty-three years I've been married, and I can honestly say that they have been the best years of my life. By and large. (*Looks around.*) I don't think she's arrived yet, so I can speak quite frankly on this score . . . They're taking a long time to get themselves married, my daughters, but I suppose this is because they're shy. Also because they never see any men. My wife doesn't like entertaining, and she finds inviting people to dinner a quite needless expense, but I can tell you in confidence . . . (*He comes down to the footlights.*) . . . my daughters can usually be found on all the major holidays at their aunt's. That's Natalya Semyonovna, the one who's got rheumatism and a yellow dress with black spots that looks as if it had cockroaches crawling over it. They'll give you something to eat there, too. And so long as my wife's not there you can, you know . . . (*Demonstrates drinking.*) I should warn you — one glass and I'm away. And then I feel so good inside myself — and so sad, all at the same time — I can't tell you what I feel like! I remember what it was like being young, and I just long to run away — oh, if you knew how much I longed to! (*Animatedly.*) Just to throw up every thing and run away with never a glance behind . . . Run where? What would it matter where? Just to get away from this mean shabby life that's turned me into the pitiful old fool I am, away from that stupid, petty, evil, evil, evil miser who's spent the last thirty-three years tormenting me, away from music and school meals and my wife's money and all this rubbish, all this vileness . . . Just to stop somewhere far, far away in the middle of the fields, just to stand there like a tree or a telegraph-pole or a scarecrow under the wide open sky and gaze all night at the shining silent moon above, just to forget, forget . . . Oh, how I should love not to remember anything! Oh, how I should love to tear off this shabby old coat I got married in thirty years ago . . . (*Tears it off.*) . . . this coat I give all these endless talks on some improving theme in . . . There, take that! (*Stamps on the coat.*) Take that! I'm old and poor and pitiful. I'm like this waistcoat—look, it's all worn out round the back. (*He demonstrates. . . .*) I don't want anything! I scorn it all! I was young once, I had brains, I went to university, I dreamed dreams, I thought I was a proper person . . . I don't want anything now! Just to be left in peace, that's all, just to be left in peace! (*Looks off, then quickly puts his coat back on.*) However, my wife's out there in the wings . . . She's arrived and she's waiting for me out there . . . (*Looks at his watch.*) We've come to the end of our time . . . If she asks you please tell her I did give the talk . . . Tell her the old dummy behaved himself properly. (*Looks off and clears his throat.*) She's looking this way . . . (*Raising his voice.*) And since, therefore, as we have just seen, tobacco contains a deadly poison, you should on no account smoke, and I hope that my little talk on 'The Evils of Tobacco' will prove to have been of some, if I may say so, use. That is all I have to say, and I am very pleased to have had the opportunity to get it off my chest.

He bows and makes a majestic exit.

The Inspector-General

The curtain in front of which The Evils of Tobacco *was
played goes up to reveal falling snow, and a cart
facing away from us.*
*Enter a STORYTELLER. As he, or she, begins to read
the story, the TRAVELLER enters. He is a middle-
aged man of entirely urban appearance, wearing
dark glasses, and a long overcoat with its collar
turned up. He is carrying a modest travelling bag. He
climbs on to the cart and sits facing us.*

STORYTELLER. The Inspector-General. In deepest in-
cognito, first by express train, then along cart-tracks and
back roads, Pyotr Pavlovich Posudin was hastening
towards the little town of N, to which he had been summoned by an anonymous letter. 'I'll take them by surprise,' he thought to himself. 'I'll come down on them
like a thunderbolt out of the blue. I can just imagine their
faces when they hear who I am . . .' (*Enter the
DRIVER, a peasant bundled up in old sacks against the
weather. He climbs up on to the cart, so that he is sitting
with his back to us, and the cart begins to trundle slowly
away from us along a pot-holed country road.*) And when
he'd thought to himself for long enough, he fell into
conversation with the driver of the cart. What did he talk
about? About himself, of course.

(*Exit the STORYTELLER.*)

TRAVELLER. I gather you've got a new Inspector-Gen-
eral in these parts.
DRIVER. True enough.
TRAVELLER. Know anything about him?

67

(*The DRIVER turns round in his seat and looks at the
TRAVELLER, who inconspicuously turns his coat
collar up a little higher.*)

DRIVER. Know anything about him? Of course we do!
We know everything about all of them up there! Every
last little clerk — we know the colour of his hair and the
size of his boots! Know about the top man? That's why
they've sent him here, so we know about him!

(*The DRIVER turns back to the front, and the TRAVEL-
LER permits himself a slight smile.*)

TRAVELLER. So, what do you reckon? Any good, is
he?

(*The DRIVER turns round and considers this.*)

DRIVER. Oh, yes, he's a good one, this one.
TRAVELLER. Really?
DRIVER. Did one good thing straight off.
TRAVELLER. What was that?
DRIVER. He got rid of the last one. Holy terror he was!
Hear him coming five mile off! Say he's going to this
little town. Somewhere like we're going, say. He'd let all
the world know about it a month before. So now he's on
his way, say, and it's like thunder and lightning coming
down the road. They're all jumping in front of him,
they're all jumping behind him, they're all jumping
either side of him. And when he gets where he's going he
has a good sleep, he has a good eat and drink — and then
he starts. Stamps his feet, shouts his head off. Then he has
another good sleep, and off he goes.
TRAVELLER. But the new one's not like that?

DRIVER. Oh, no, the new one goes everywhere on the quiet, like. Creeps round like a cat. Don't want no one to see him, don't want no one to know who he is. Say he's going to this town down the road here. Someone there sent him a letter on the sly, let's say. 'Things going on here you should know about.' Something of that kind. Well, now, he creeps out of his office, so none of them up there see him go. He hops on a train just like anyone else, just like you or me. Then when he gets off he don't go jumping into a cab or nothing fancy. Oh, no. An ordinary horse and cart will do for him! He wraps himself up from head to toe so you can't see his face, and he wheezes away like an old dog so no one can recognise his voice.

TRAVELLER. Wheezes? That's not wheezing! That's the way he talks! So I gather.

DRIVER. Oh, is it? But the tales they tell about him. You'd laugh till you burst your tripes!

TRAVELLER. (*sourly*) I'm sure I should.

DRIVER. Drinks, mind!

TRAVELLER. (*startled*) Drinks?

DRIVER. Oh, like a hole in the ground. Famous for it.

TRAVELLER. He's never touched a drop! I mean, from what I've heard.

DRIVER. Oh, not in public, no. Goes to some great ball—'No thank you, not for me.' Oh, no, he puts it away at home! Wakes up in the morning, rubs his eyes, and the first thing he does he shouts, 'Vodka!' So in runs his valet with a glass. 'And another!' says he. Fixed himself up a tube behind his desk, he has. Leans down, takes a pull on it, no one the wiser.

TRAVELLER. (*offended*) How do you know all this, may I ask?

DRIVER. Can't hide it from the servants, can you? The valet and the coachman have got tongues in their heads. Then again, he's on the road, say, going about his business—and he keeps the bottle in his little bag. (*The TRAVELLER discreetly pushes his travelling bag out of the DRIVER's sight.*) It's the same with his women.

TRAVELLER. (*startled*) His women?

DRIVER. Oh, he's a devil for the women, this one! Ten of them, he's got!

TRAVELLER. Ten? That's absolute nonsense! I mean . . . surely . . . ?

DRIVER. He's got two of them living in the house! One of them, they say she's the housekeeper—that's Nastasya Ivanovna. The other one—what's her name, now? Forget my own name next . . . Ludmila Semyonovna —she's supposed to be some sort of clerk. But Nastasya —she's the top one. Whatever she wants she's only to say and he does it. Runs circles round him, she does, like a fox round his tail. She's the one who wears the trousers. The people aren't half so frightened of him as what they are of her. Now, Number Three, she lives on Kachalnaya Street. Public scandal, that one, because her husband's niece by his first wife—she's Number Four . . . !

TRAVELLER. Yes, yes, quite, quite . . . But at least he's good at his job, you say?

DRIVER. Oh, he's a blessing from heaven, I'll grant him that.

TRAVELLER. Very cunning—you were saying.

DRIVER. Oh, he creeps around all right.

TRAVELLER. And then he pounces, yes? I should think some people must get the surprise of their life, mustn't they?

DRIVER. No, no—let's be fair, now. Give him his due. He don't make no trouble.

TRAVELLER. No, I mean, if no one know he's coming . . .

DRIVER. Oh, that's what *he* thinks! Oh, Lord bless you — *we* all know!

TRAVELLER. You know?

DRIVER. Oh, some gentleman gets off the train at the station back there with his greatcoat up to his eyebrows and says, 'No, I don't want a cab, thank you, I don't want nothing fancy, just an ordinary horse and cart for me' — well, we'd put two and two together, wouldn't we! Say it was you, now, creeping along down the road here. The lads would be down there in a cab by now! By the time you got there the whole town would be as regular as clockwork! And you'd think to yourself, 'Oh, look at that! As clean as a whistle! And they didn't know I was coming!' No, that's why he's such a blessing after the other one. This one believes it!

TRAVELLER. Oh, I see.

DRIVER. What, you thought we wouldn't know him? Why, we've got the electric telegraph these days! Take today, now. I'm going past the station back there this morning, and the fellow who runs the buffet comes out like a bolt of lightning. Arms full of baskets and bottles. 'Where are you off to?' I say. 'Doing drinks and refreshments for the Inspector-General!' he says, and he jumps into a post-chaise and goes flying off down the road here. So there's the old Inspector-General, all muffled up like a roll of carpet, going secretly along in a cart somewhere — and when he gets there, nothing to be seen but vodka and cold salmon!

TRAVELLER. (*shouts*) Right — turn round, then, damn you!

DRIVER. (*to the horse*) Whoa, boy! Whoa! (*To the TRAVELLER.*) Oh, so what's this, then? Don't want to go running into the Inspector-General, is that it?

(The TRAVELLER gestures impatiently to the DRIVER to turn the cart round.)

(To the horse.) Back we go, then, boy. Home we go.

(The DRIVER turns the cart round, and the TRAVELLER tips back his head and takes a swig from his travelling bag.)

Though if I know the old devil, he's like as not turned round and gone home again himself.

Blackout.

Swan Song

Enter STAGEHANDS, who strike the set of The Inspector-General *by working lights. Enter two
ACTRESSES, putting on their overcoats to go home.
As the set goes, it reveals the empty stage of a second-
rate provincial theatre at night.*

FIRST ACTRESS. *Swan Song.* Scene: the stage of a small
provincial theatre. They've been doing a benefit evening
for one of the older actors. There were curtain calls and
bouquets. Then drinks and speeches and toasts. Now
everyone's gone home.

*(She begins to go off. The STAGEHANDS finish their
work and depart, whistling. One by one the working
lights go off.)*

SECOND ACTRESS. The theatre's empty. Night.
Darkness.
FIRST ACTRESS. *(calls, off)* Nina!

*(The SECOND ACTRESS goes off, too. There is a noise
of a heavy door slamming, off, and of a key turning in
the lock. For a moment there is silence. Then the
door at the back of the stage opens, and SVETLOVI-
DOV, an elderly comic actor, enters holding a candle. He laughs.)*

SVETLOVIDOV. Well, here's a fine how-do-you-do!
Here's a fine state of affairs! Fell asleep in my dressing-
room! The show finished hours ago — everyone's gone
home — and what am I doing? — I'm quietly taking forty
winks! Oh, you stupid old so-and-so! You silly old devil!

Must have got so tight I dropped off as I sat there. There's a bright thing to do. (*Calls.*) Yegorka! Yegorka, damn you! Petrushka! They've gone to bed, the devils. Damn them, the pair of them. Yegorka! (*Picks up the stool, sits down on it, and puts the candle on the floor.*) Silence. No answer but the echoes. I tipped them three rubles apiece today—you won't find them now for love nor money. Off they went, the swine, and I presume locked up after them. (*Twists his head back and forth.*) Drunk! Ugh! And all because it was my benefit night . . . My God, how much of that vodka and beer did I get down me? My whole body feels like the bottom of a parrot's cage. I've got twelve tongues sleeping rough inside my mouth . . . Horrible . . . (*Pause.*) How stupid . . . The old fool's got drunk and he doesn't even know himself what it was all in aid of . . . Oh, heavens above! My back's breaking, my head's splitting, I've got the shivers, and I feel as cold and dark inside me as the grave. Even if you don't care about your health you might at least take a little pity on your old age, you stupid clown. (*Pause.*) Old age. Oh yes, you can get up to your tricks, you can put a brave face on it and play the fool, but your life's over. Sixty-eight years you've kissed goodbye to now, for heaven's sake! You won't see them again. The whole bottle drunk—only the last drop left at the bottom . . . Only the dregs . . . So there we are. That's the way it is. Like it or not, it's time to rehearse the part of the corpse. Old father death is waiting in the wings . . . (*Gazes out front.*) I've been on the stage for forty-five years, though, and I do believe this is the first time I've ever seen a theatre in the middle of the night. I do believe it is . . . Curious . . . (*Comes down to the footlights.*) Can't see a thing . . . Just make out the

dome . . . and the box there . . . Everything else—
blackness! A black, bottomless pit, like the tomb, with
death hiding in it . . . Brr! Cold! There's a draught
from out there like the draught from an empty fire-
place . . . Just the spot to raise a few ghosts! God, but
you can feel the fear strike into you . . . My spine's
crawling . . . (*Calls.*) Yegorka! Petrushka! Where are
you, damn you? My God, though, what am I doing
swearing like this? Give up swearing, for God's sake!
Give up drinking! You're an old man! It's time to die!
People get up in the morning and go to church when
they're sixty-eight, they get ready for death. And what are
you doing? Swearing, drunk as a pig, tricked out in this
clown's costume . . . I'm not fit to be seen! Better go
and get dressed . . . Oh, it's eerie! If I stay here all night
like this I might die of fright . . .

(*He goes towards his dressing-room. As he does so,
NIKITA IVANICH appears from behind a pile of
props, wearing a white dressing-gown. At the sight
of him SVETLOVIDOV cries out in terror and
cowers back.*)

SVETLOVIDOV. Who's that? What is it? Who do you
want? (*Stamps his feet.*) Who is it?

NIKITA. It's me, sir!

SVETLOVIDOV. Who?

NIKITA. (*slowly coming towards him*) Me, sir. Nikita
Ivanich. The prompter. Me, sir!

SVETLOVIDOV. (*sinks helplessly on to the stool,
breathing heavily and shaking all over.*) Good God! It's
who? It's you? Is it? Nikitushka? What on earth are you
doing here?

NIKITA. I sleep here, sir. You won't tell anyone, sir, will you. I haven't got anywhere else to go, so help me God.

SVETLOVIDOV. You, is it, Nikitushka . . . Good God, good God! We took sixteen curtains, we got three bouquets and a lot else besides, everyone was in ecstasies —and no one could wake up a poor drunken old man and take him home . . . I'm an old man, Nikitushka! I'm sixty-eight. I'm ill. My poor sick heart's fading away . . . (*Seizes NIKITA IVANICH's hand and weeps.*) Don't leave me, Nikitushka! I'm old, I've no strength left, I've got to die . . . I'm frightened, I'm frightened!

NIKITA. (*gently and respectfully*) Time you were going home, Vasily Vasilich.

SVETLOVIDOV. I'm not going! I've no home to go to! No home! No home!

NIKITA. God save us, forgotten where you live now, have you?

SVETLOVIDOV. I don't want to go home! I'm all on my own there. I haven't got anyone in the world, Nikitushka. No family, no wife, no children. I'm as lonely as the wind in the fields. I've no one to remember me when I'm gone. I get frightened on my own. No one to warm me when I'm cold, no one to be nice to me, no one to put me to bed when I'm drunk. Who do I belong to? Who needs me? Who loves me? No one loves me, Nikitushka!

NIKITA. (*on the verge of tears*) The audience loves you, Vasily Vasilich!

SVETLOVIDOV. The audience has gone home and gone to bed and forgotten all about its clown! No, no one needs me, no one loves me . . . No wife, no children . . .

NIKITA. Nonsense, now, what are you grieving about?

SVETLOVIDOV. I'm human, aren't I? I'm alive? I've got blood flowing in my veins, not water? I'm a gentleman, Nikitushka, I come from a good family. Before I fell into this pit I served in the army — I was in the artillery. And what a fine young fellow I was! What a handsome young, upright young, dashing young, fiery young fellow I was! My God, though, where's it all gone? But what an actor I became then! Didn't I, Nikitushka, didn't I? (*He gets up, leaning on NIKITA IVANICH's arm.*) Where's it all gone, that time, where is it now? Lord, Lord . . . I looked out into that pit tonight, and it all came back to me, it all came back! That pit out there has swallowed up forty-five years of my life. And what a life it's been, Nikitushka! I look out into that pit now and I see it all down to the last little thing, I see it like your face in front of me. The delights of youth — the faith, the fire — the love of women! Ah, the women, Nikitushka!

NIKITA. Time you were in bed, Vasily Vasilich.

SVETLOVIDOV. When I was a young actor, when I was just starting to get my teeth into it, I remember there was a woman who loved me for my art. An elegant creature she was, as graceful as a poplar, as young and innocent, as pure and passionate, as a summer dawn! One glance from her blue eyes, one flash of her amazing smile, and no darkness could resist. The waves of the sea break against the rocks, but the waves of her hair would have broken cliffs and melted icebergs. I remember one day standing in front of her as I'm standing in front of you now . . . She was lovelier than ever that day, and she gave me a look I shall remember in my grave . . . All the sweetness, softness, profundity and brilliance of youth! Intoxicated with happiness, I fell on my knees before her and asked her to marry me. (*Lowering his voice.*) And what did she say? She said, 'Give up the stage!' Give—up—the stage! Do you see? She didn't mind being in love with an actor, but *marry* one? Not on your life! I was appearing that day, I remember. A low comic part. And as I performed I felt as if my eyes had been opened. I saw that there was no sacred art about it—that it was all delirium and delusion—that I was other people's creature, the plaything of their idle fancy, their jester, their buffoon! And I saw the audience for what it was! From then on I didn't trust their applause or their bouquets or their ecstasies. Oh yes, Nikitushka! They applaud me, they pay a ruble for my photograph, but they don't see me as someone like themselves. They see me as trash, as something not much better than a courtesan. They scrape acquaintance with me so they can boast about it, but they wouldn't demean themselves by marrying their sisters or daughters to me. I don't trust them! (*Sinks down on to the stool.*) Don't trust them an inch!

NIKITA. You don't look yourself, Vasily Vasilich! You've got me frightened now. Let's go home, for the love of God.

SVETLOVIDOV. I grew up that day. And dear it cost me, Nikitushka! After that little incident . . . after *her* . . . I lost all sense of aim and direction, I stumbled on without looking where I was going. I played fools and scoffers, I clowned, I sowed corruption—yet what an artist I was, what a talent I had! I buried that talent, I cheapened myself. I coarsened my language, I lost the divine image and likeness. That black pit opened its jaws and swallowed me up! I've never felt it before, but to-night . . . I woke up and looked back, and there were sixty-eight years behind me. Old age! I saw it tonight for the first time. My song is sung! (*Sobs.*) My race is run!

NIKITA. There now, Vasily Vasilich! There now!

Don't take on so. Oh, Lord in heaven! (*Calls.*) Petrushka! Yegorka!

SVETLOVIDOV. But what a talent I had! What power! You can't imagine! What diction, how much feeling and grace, what a range of emotion inside this breast! (*He strikes his chest.*) I was overpowering! Listen, listen . . . Wait, let me get my breath . . . *King Lear,* say . . . The sky black, rain, thunder — boom, boom! — lightning striping the blackness — zzzz! — then:

Blow, winds, and crack your cheeks! rage! blow!
You cataracts and hurricanoes, spout
Till you have drench'd our steeples, drown'd the cocks!
You sulphurous and thought-executing fires,
Vaunt-couriers to oak-cleaving thunderbolts,
Singe my white head! And thou, all-shaking thunder,
Smite flat the thick rotundity o'the world!
Crack nature's moulds, all germens spill at once
That make ingrateful man!

(*impatiently*) Quick, the Fool! (*Stamps his feet.*) Come on, come on, the Fool's lines! Quick, quick!

NIKITA. (*as the FOOL*) O nuncle, court holy-water in a dry house is better than this rain-water out o'door. Good nuncle, in, and ask thy daughters' blessing: here's a night pities neither wise man nor fool.

SVETLOVIDOV.
Rumble thy bellyful! Spit, fire! spout, rain!
Nor rain, wind, thunder, fire are my daughters:
I tax not you, you elements, with unkindness;
I never gave you kingdom, call'd you children . . .

The power there! The talent! The artistry! Where's all this damned old age, then? Not a sign of it! Old age? Nonsense! Old age? Rubbish! Power, pumping like a

fountain out of every vein! Youth, Nikitushka! Fresh-
ness! Life! Where you've got talent there's no room for
old age! Have I gone mad, Nikitushka? Are these mere
ravings? (*The sound of doors being opened, off.*) What
was that?

NIKITA. Petrushka and Yegorka must have come
back . . . No, you've got the talent, Vasily Vasilich!
You've got the talent!

SVETLOVIDOV. (*calls, in the direction of the banging
doors*) In here, you drunkards! (*To NIKITA IVANICH.*)
We'll go and get dressed . . . Old age? No such thing!
Stuff and nonsense . . . (*Laughs cheerfully.*) What are
you crying about? My dear old idiot, what's all this sniv-
elling for? Come on, now, that's enough of that. What's
that face for? come on, come on. (*He puts his arm
around NIKITA IVANICH, on the verge of tears himself.*) You mustn't cry. Where you've got art, where
you've got talent, there's no room for old age, there's no
room for loneliness or being ill. Even death's only half
itself. (*Weeps.*) No, you're right, Nikitushka, our song is
sung, our race is run. What talent do I have? I'm a
squeezed lemon, a melting icicle, a rusty nail. And what
are you? A prompter, an old theatre rat . . . Off we go,
then. (*They begin to move off.*)
What talent do I have? All I'm good for in serious plays is
an attendant lord . . . and I'm getting old for
that . . . Yes . . . You remember that speech in *Othello*, Nikitushka?
O, now for ever
Farewell the tranquil mind! farewell content!
Farewell the plumed troop, and the big wars
That make ambition virtue! Oh, farewell,
Farewell the neighing steed, and the shrill trump,

The spirit-stirring drum, the ear-piercing fife,
The royal banner and all quality,
Pride, pomp and circumstance of glorious war!

NIKITA. You've got the talent, Vasily Vasilich! You've got the talent!
SVETLOVIDOV.
And you, O you mortal engines, whose rude throats
Th'immortal Jove's dread clamours counterfeit,
Farewell! Othello's occupation's gone!

(*Exit, with NIKITA IVANICH.*)

Blackout.

The Proposal

Enter SERVANTS, who furnish a drawing-room on a country estate.

A Servant. *The Proposal.*

(*Exeunt the SERVANTS. Enter CHUBUKOV, a landowner, and LOMOV, his plump, healthy, but very hypochondriacal neighbour. LOMOV is wearing tails and white gloves.*)

CHUBUKOV. My dear fellow! Of all the people in the world! What a pleasure! What a surprise! My dear, dear fellow! How have you been keeping?

LOMOV. Oh . . . Thank you. And you, if I may ask?

CHUBUKOV. Oh, we keep quietly toddling along . . . Sustained by your prayers, and all the rest of it. Have a seat, I do most humbly beseech you . . . So good of you to remember your neighbours. But my dear good chap, why so formal? Tails, gloves, and all the rest of it? Not on your way somewhere, are you?

LOMOV. Only here, my dear Stepan Stepanich.

CHUBUKOV. Then why the tails, my dear old chap? It looks like New Year's Eve!

LOMOV. The thing is this. (*Takes him by the arm.*) I have a certain request to make. My dear Stepan Stepanich, this is not the first time I have had the honour of asking for your help, and you have always been — how shall I put it . . . ? I'm sorry, I'm getting myself all worked up. My dear Stepan Stepanich . . . I'll just have a drink of water. (*Drinks water.*)

CHUBUKOV. (*aside*) He's after money! He's not getting any! (*To Lomov.*) So what's the trouble, then, my dear old fellow?

LOMOV. The thing is this, my dear my dear Stepanich . . . ah, Stepan Stepan Mydearich . . . I'm getting myself into a terrible state, as you can see . . . To put it in a nutshell, you're the only person who can help me, although of course I've done nothing to deserve it and . . . and I've not the slightest right to expect it . . .

CHUBUKOV. My dear good chap, don't prolong the agony! Get it off your chest! What is it?

LOMOV. Here we are, then. Without more ado. The thing is that I have come to ask for the hand of your daughter in marriage.

CHUBUKOV. (*joyfully*) My dear dear dear dear fellow! Ivan Vasilyevich! Say it again—I'm not sure I heard aright . . .

LOMOV. I have the honour to ask for the . . .

CHUBUKOV. (*interrupts him*) My dear dear dear dear dear dear fellow! I'm so delighted, and all the rest of it! Tickled to death, et cetera et cetera! (*Embraces and kisses him.*) Long been my dearest wish. (*Sheds a tear.*) My dear good dear old fellow! Always loved you like a son. God send you both love and harmony and all the rest of it. So looked forward to this day . . . ! But why am I standing here like a complete imbecile? I'm stunned with joy, absolutely stunned! Oh, my heartfelt, heartfelt . . . I'll go and call her, et cetera et cetera.

LOMOV. (*touched*) What do you think, my dear Stepan Stepanich—can I count on her acceptance?

CHUBUKOV. A handsome young fellow like yourself —look at you!—and she's going to up and say no? I should think she's as mad as a kitten about you, and so on . . . Stay there!

(*Exit CHUBUKOV.*)

Lomov. (*alone*) Freezing . . . I'm shivering all over. Examination fever. Take the plunge—that's the main thing. Never get married if you keep thinking about it, keep hesitating, keep talking about it, keep waiting for some ideal love, some real love . . . Brrr . . . So cold! Natalya Stepanovna knows how to run a house, she's not bad-looking, she's educated . . . what more do I want? It's just that I'm in such a state I've got my buzzing in the ears coming on. (*Drinks water.*) I can't not get married, after all . . . In the first place I'm 35—what people call the critical age. On top of which I need a regular, well-ordered life . . . I've got a weak heart—I keep having palpitations. I fly up easily—I'm always getting into a state about things . . . Here I am now—I've got a tremble in my lip and a twitch in my right eyelid . . . But the worst thing is trying to sleep. I get into bed, and I'm just starting to drop off when I get this sudden thing in my left side—woomph!—and it goes straight up into my shoulder and head . . . I jump out of bed like a lunatic, I walk up and down for a bit, I lie down again, I'm just starting to drop off, when suddenly, in my left side again—woomph! If it happens once it happens a dozen time . . .

(*Enter NATALYA STEPANOVNA.*)

Natalya Stepanovna. Oh, good Lord, it's you! Papa said, 'There's a man come to collect some goods.' Ivan Vasilyevich . . .

Lomov. My dear Natalya Stepanovna!

Natalya Stepanovna. Oh, and in my pinny, look—all any old how . . . We're podding the peas for dry-ing. Why haven't we seen you for so long? Have a seat . . . (*They sit.*) Do you want some lunch?

LOMOV. I have eaten, thank you.

NATALYA STEPANOVNA. Do smoke if you want to . . . Matches, look . . . Wonderful weather. Such rain yesterday, though! The men didn't do a stroke all day. How much have you got in? Can you imagine, I just went guzzle guzzle — mowed the entire meadow. Now I'm regretting it. Frightened all my hay's going to rot. Should have waited. What's all this, though? Tails? Never thought I'd live to see you in tails! Off to a ball, are you? You're looking very handsome today, I must say . . . Why are you all dressed up like this?

LOMOV. (*growing agitated*) Now, my dear Natalya Stepanovna . . . The thing is this. I have decided to ask you to . . . to listen to what I have to say. Now, this will of course come as something of a surprise — you may even be rather cross about it — but the point is this . . . (*Aside.*) So hideously cold!

NATALYA STEPANOVNA. What is it, then? (*Pause.*) Go on.

LOMOV. I shall be as brief as I can. You know, of course, my dear Natalya Stepanovna, that I have had the honour of being acquainted with your family for a long time — since I was a child. My dear departed aunt and her husband, from whom, as I believe you know, I inherited my estate, always had the greatest respect for your father and your dear departed mother. We Lomovs and you Chubukovs have always been on very friendly — one might almost say family — terms. My land, moreover, as you know, marches with yours. My Ox Lea Meadows abut your birchwoods. We have always helped each other out with the haymaking . . .

NATALYA STEPANOVNA. Sorry, but I'm going to interrupt you. You say '*My* Ox Lea Meadows.' Not yours, surely?

LOMOV. Mine, I think, yes.

NATALYA STEPANOVNA. Goodness gracious! Ox Lea Meadows are ours, not yours!

LOMOV. I think not, my dear Natalya Stepanovna. I think mine.

NATALYA STEPANOVNA. This is news to me. How do they come to be yours?

LOMOV. How do you mean, how? I'm talking about the Ox Lea Meadows that make a wedge between your birchwoods and Burnt Swamp.

NATALYA STEPANOVNA. Exactly. They're ours.

LOMOV. No, you're wrong, my dear Natalya Stepanovna — they're mine.

NATALYA STEPANOVNA. Oh, come, now, Ivan Vasilyevich. Since when have they been yours?

LOMOV. Since when? They've always been ours, to the best of my recollection.

NATALYA STEPANOVNA. I'm sorry, but really!

LOMOV. My dear Natalya Stepanovna, it's all there in the documents. The ownership was at one time in dispute, that's true. But now everyone knows they're mine. There's no dispute about it. I think you'll find that my aunt's grandmother granted the use of the meadows, rent-free for an unspecified period of time, to your father's grandfather's peasants in consideration of their making bricks for her. Your father's grandfather's peasants enjoyed this rent-free use of the meadows for some forty years and became accustomed to regard them as their own. But then, when the land register was published . . .

NATALYA STEPANOVNA. It's not like that at all! My father and my great-grandfather both regarded their land as extending right up to Burnt Swamp—so Ox Lea Meadows were ours. What possible dispute can there be? I don't understand. I find all this rather vexing!

LOMOV. I'll show you the documents!

NATALYA STEPANOVNA. No, it's just your little joke, isn't it. Or else you're having me on. It's rather a shock, that's all. We own a piece of land for nearly three hundred years, and suddenly we're informed it's not ours! I'm sorry, but I can scarcely believe my ears . . . It's not the meadows I mind about. A dozen acres all told—they're not worth more than three hundred rubles or so. It's the unfairness of it that outrages me. Say what you like, but I cannot abide unfairness.

LOMOV. Listen to what I'm saying, I implore you! Your father's grandfather's peasants, as I have, I believe, already said, made bricks for my aunt's grandmother. My aunt's grandmother, wishing to do them a favour in return . . .

NATALYA STEPANOVNA. Aunts—grandmothers— grandfathers I don't know what you're talking about! All I know is that the meadows are ours!

LOMOV. Excuse me, but they're mine!

NATALYA STEPANOVNA. Ours! You can stand there arguing all day—you can put on fifteen lots of tails— but they're ours, ours, ours! I've no wish to take what's yours and no great desire to lose what's mine, thank you very much!

LOMOV. It's not that I *want* the meadows—it's the principle of the thing. If *you* want them—please—I'll give you them.

NATALYA STEPANOVNA. *I* can perfectly well give them to *you*, for that matter, since they're mine! This is all very strange, to say the least. We've always thought of you as a good neighbour, as a friend. Last year we lent you our threshing-machine, which meant that we had to finish threshing our corn in November. And here you are treating us as if we were Gypsies! Giving me my own land! I'm sorry, but that's not very neighbourly! I think it's downright impertinence, if you want to know, . . .

LOMOV. So you're telling me I'm some kind of land-grabber, are you? Madam, never in my life have I laid a finger upon another man's land, and no one is going to make such an accusation with impunity. (*Moves rapidly across to the carafe and drinks water.*) Ox Lea Meadows are mine!

NATALYA STEPANOVNA. You're a liar! They're ours!

LOMOV. Mine!

NATALYA STEPANOVNA. Liar! I'm going to prove it to you! I'm going to send my men straight down there today to mow them!

LOMOV. You're what?

NATALYA STEPANOVNA. My men, today — they'll be down there mowing them!

LOMOV. I'll throw them out on their necks!

NATALYA STEPANOVNA. You wouldn't dare!

LOMOV. (*clutching at his heart*) Ox Lea Meadows are mine! You understand? Mine!

NATALYA STEPANOVNA. Don't shout at me, thank you! You can shout and wheeze with rage at home, but while you're here I must ask you to keep yourself under control!

LOMOV. If I were not in terrible agony with these palpitations, madam, if the blood were not pounding in my temples, I should take a very different tone with you! (*Shouts.*) Ox Lea Meadows are mine!

NATALYA STEPANOVNA. They're ours!

LOMOV. They're mine!

NATALYA STEPANOVNA. They're ours!

LOMOV. They're mine!

(*Enter CHUBUKOV.*)

CHUBUKOV. What? What? What? What's all this shouting?

NATALYA STEPANOVNA. Papa, explain to this gentleman, will you, who Ox Lea Meadows belongs to — us or him?

CHUBUKOV. (*to LOMOV*) My dear fellow, they're ours!

LOMOV. Excuse me, Stepan Stepanich, but how do they come to be yours? Don't *you* start being unreasonable as well! My aunt's grandmother granted temporary rent-free use of the meadows to your grandfather's peasants. The peasants enjoyed this use of the land for forty years and became accustomed to regard it as their own. But when the register was published . . .

CHUBUKOV. My dear sweet man, forgive me. You're forgetting that the peasants didn't pay your aunt's grandmother, and all the rest of it, precisely because at that time the ownership of the meadows was in dispute, et cetera et cetera. But the point is that now, as any fool knows, they're ours. You obviously haven't seen the land register!

LOMOV. But I can prove to you they're mine!

CHUBUKOV. My dear darling man, you can't!

LOMOV. I can!

CHUBUKOV. Dearest heart, why are you shouting like this? You won't prove anything by shouting. I've no wish to take what's yours, and absolutely no intention at all of giving up what's mine. Why should I? If it came right down to it, and you were absolutely determined to lay claim to the meadows, then, my dear sweet dear dear darling fellow, I should sooner give it to the peasants than you. So there!

LOMOV. I don't understand! What right do you have to give away other people's property?

CHUBUKOV. I'll be the judge of what right I have, thank you very much. And by the by, young man, I'm not used to having that tone taken with me, and all the rest of it. I'm twice as old as you are, young man, and I'll thank you to keep a civil tongue in your head, et cetera et cetera.

LOMOV. No, but you just take me for a fool, don't you — you think you can laugh at me. You call my land yours — and then you expect me to keep calm and talk to you politely! That's not the way good neighbours should behave! You're not a neighbour — you're a landgrabber!

CHUBUKOV. What was that? What did you say?

NATALYA STEPANOVNA. Papa, go straight out and send the men down to mow the meadows!

CHUBUKOV. (to LOMOV) What was that you said, my dear sir?

NATALYA STEPANOVNA. Ox Lea Meadows are ours, and I won't ever give them up, I won't, I won't!

LOMOV. We'll see about that! I'm going to prove to you in court that they're mine.

CHUBUKOV. In court? Well might you go to court, my dear sir! Well might you! I know you! This is precisely what you've been waiting for, a chance to go to court, and all the rest of it. You're a born troublemaker! All your family were! Troublemakers, the lot of them!

LOMOV. I'll thank you not to insult my family! The Lomovs have all been honest citizens. None of them has ever been taken to court for embezzlement, like your uncle!

CHUBUKOV. No, but the Lomovs have all been mad!

NATALYA STEPANOVNA. All of them! All of them! All of them!

CHUBUKOV. Your grandfather drank like a fish, and all the rest of it, and this famous aunt of yours—her younger sister ran off with an architect!

LOMOV. And your mother was deformed! (*Clutches at his heart.*) Woomph!—in my side! Feel the blood rushing to my head! Oh, my heavens! Water, water!

CHUBUKOV. And your father did nothing but gorge and gamble!

NATALYA STEPANOVNA. And your aunt was the biggest gossip in the neighbourhood!

LOMOV. My left leg's paralysed . . . And as for you, you underhand schemer . . . Oh, my heart . . . ! Everyone knows what you were up to at the elections . . . I've got spots before the eyes . . . Where's my hat?

NATALYA STEPANOVNA. How low! How dishonourable! How vile!

CHUBUKOV. What about you, then, you two-faced conniving snake-in-the-grass! Yes, sir—you, sir!

LOMOV. Hat . . . Heart . . . Which way am I going? Where's the door? Oh, I think I'm dying . . . Can't pick my foot up . . . (*Goes to the door.*)

CHUBUKOV. (*following him*) Then drag it out after you and don't ever bring it back!

NATALYA STEPANOVNA. Take us to court! We'll see what happens!

(*LOMOV stumbles out.*)

CHUBUKOV. So much for him! (*Walks up and down in agitation.*)

NATALYA STEPANOVNA. So much for good neighbours!

CHUBUKOV. The scoundrel! The scarecrow!

NATALYA STEPANOVNA. The monster! Takes your land — then turns round and curses you!

CHUBUKOV. And you know what? This hobgoblin, this walking blight, has the cheek to come here and propose! How about that?

NATALYA STEPANOVNA. Propose? How do you mean, propose?

CHUBUKOV. How do I mean, propose? I mean he came here to propose to you!

NATALYA STEPANOVNA. To propose? To me? Why on earth didn't you say so before?

CHUBUKOV. Got himself up in his tails to do it! The stupid little sausage!

NATALYA STEPANOVNA. He was going to propose to me? Ah! (*Falls into the armchair and moans.*) Get him back! Ah! Get him back! Get him back!

CHUBUKOV. Get him back?

NATALYA STEPANOVNA. Quick, quick! I'm going to faint! Get him back! (*Has hysterics.*)

CHUBUKOV. What is it? What's the matter? (*Clutches his head.*) Oh, what a wretched fate is mine! I'll shoot myself! I'll hang myself! They're all driving me mad!

NATALYA STEPANOVNA. I'm dying! Get him back!

CHUBUKOV. All right! I'll get him! Don't howl! (*Runs out.*)

NATALYA STEPANOVNA. (*alone, moaning*) What have we done? What have we done? Get him back!

CHUBUKOV. (*runs back in*) He's coming, he's coming! You'll have to talk to him yourself — I'm damned if I'm going to.

NATALYA STEPANOVNA. (*moaning*) Get him back!

CHUBUKOV. (*shouting*) I've told you—he's coming! Oh, Lord in heaven, what a profession, being the father of a grown-up daughter! I'll cut my throat! I will—I'll cut my throat! We've cursed the fellow uphill and down, we've shamed him, we've thrown him out—and you're the one who did it! Yes, you!

NATALYA STEPANOVNA. Me? It was you!

CHUBUKOV. Oh, of course, it was all my fault! (*LOMOV appears in the doorway.*) Well, you talk to him yourself!

(*Exit CHUBUKOV.*)

LOMOV. (*enters, in an exhausted state*) Terrible palpitations . . . My leg's gone numb . . . Pain in my side . . .

NATALYA STEPANOVNA. Forgive me, we became a little heated . . . I remember now—Ox Lea Meadows *are* yours.

LOMOV. My heart's beating like a drum . . . Mine, the Meadows, yes . . . I've got a twitch in both eyelids . . .

NATALYA STEPANOVNA. Yours, the Meadows, yours, yours. Have a seat, do . . . (*They sit.*) Yes, we were wrong.

LOMOV. It was just the principle of the thing. I don't care about the land, but I do care about the principle of the thing . . .

NATALYA STEPANOVNA. The principle—exactly . . . But let's talk about something else.

LOMOV. Particularly since I have *proof*. My aunt's grandmother granted your father's grandfather's peasants . . .

NATALYA STEPANOVNA. Yes, yes, yes . . . (*To LOMOV.*) Shall you be going hunting again soon?

LOMOV. For blackcock, yes — I'm hoping to start after the harvest. Oh, but have you heard? Such bad luck. You remember Finder? He's gone lame.

NATALYA STEPANOVNA. Oh, no! How did that happen?

LOMOV. No idea . . . He must have dislocated something or got bitten by the other dogs. (*Sighs.*) My best dog, not to mention the money! You know I paid 125 rubles for him?

NATALYA STEPANOVNA. Oh, too much, Ivan Vasilyevich, too much!

LOMOV. I thought it was a bargain. He's a wonderful dog.

NATALYA STEPANOVNA. Papa got Flyer for 85 rubles, and after all, Flyer's a vastly better dog than Finder.

LOMOV. Flyer? Better than Finder? What do you mean? (*Laughs.*) Flyer is better than Finder?

NATALYA STEPANOVNA. Well, of course he is! Flyer's young, certainly, he's not out of his puppy coat yet, but in his line, in his action, you won't find a better dog in the country.

LOMOV. Forgive me, but you're forgetting his jaw, surely. He's undershot, and undershot dogs always have a poor bite!

NATALYA STEPANOVNA. Undershot? First I've heard of it!

LOMOV. I assure you — his bottom jaw's shorter than his top jaw.

NATALYA STEPANOVNA. You've measured them, have you?

LOMOV. Yes — I've measured them! He's all right for coursing, certainly, but when it comes to holding, well . . .

NATALYA STEPANOVNA. In the first place, Flyer is a pure-bred borzoi, by Harness out of Chiseller, whereas heaven alone knows where your spotty mongrel sprang from. In the second place, your dog is as old as the hills and as ugly as sin.

LOMOV. Old he may be, but I shouldn't swap him for five of your Flyers. What?—Finder's a dog—Flyer's a—well, it's ridiculous! Dogs like that—they're as common as dirt—every little whipper-in's got one. 25 rubles at the outside.

NATALYA STEPANOVNA. There's some demon of contradiction got into you today, Ivan Vasilyevich. First you claim the Meadows are yours, then you claim Finder's better than Flyer. I can't bear people who won't say what they really think. You know perfectly well that Flyer's a hundred times better than that stupid Finder of years, so why say the opposite?

LOMOV. You obviously think I'm blind or stupid. Can't you understand that Flyer is undershot?

NATALYA STEPANOVNA. He's not.

LOMOV. He's undershot!

NATALYA STEPANOVNA. (*shouts*) He's not!

LOMOV. Then why are you shouting, madam?

NATALYA STEPANOVNA. Why are you talking nonsense? It's absolutely outrageous! Your Finder is ready to be put down, and here you are comparing him with Flyer!

LOMOV. I'm sorry, but I can pursue this debate no further. I am suffering from palpitations of the heart.

NATALYA STEPANOVNA. I've noticed with sportsmen that the ones who talk most are the ones who have least idea what they're talking about.

LOMOV. Be quiet, madam, I beg of you. I'm about to have a heart attack . . . (*Shouts.*) Be quiet!

NATALYA STEPANOVNA. I shan't be quiet until you

admit that Flyer is a hundred times better than your Finder!

LOMOV. He isn't — he's a hundred times worse! I hope he drops dead! Oh, my head . . . my eyes . . . my shoulder . . .

NATALYA STEPANOVNA. Yes, well, there's no need for your Finder to drop dead, because he's dead already!

LOMOV. (*weeps*) Be quiet, will you! I'm having a heart attack!

NATALYA STEPANOVNA. I won't be quiet!

(*Enter CHUBUKOV.*)

CHUBUKOV. *Now* what's happening?

NATALYA STEPANOVNA. Papa, just tell us frankly, in all honesty. Which is the better dog — our Flyer or his Finder?

LOMOV. Stepan Stepanich, I implore you, just tell us one thing. Is Flyer undershot or is he not? Yes or no?

CHUBUKOV. What if he is? What does it matter? There still isn't a better dog in the whole district, and all the rest of it.

LOMOV. But in fact my Finder's better, isn't he. In all honesty!

CHUBUKOV. Don't get excited, my dear fellow. Listen. Your Finder has his points, by all means. He's pure-bred, he's strong on his feet, and he's got a good fallaway. But, my dear dear fellow, if you want to know the truth, that dog has two bad faults. He's old, and he has a short muzzle.

LOMOV. I'm sorry, I'm having palpitations of the heart . . . Let's just look at the facts . . . In Maruskin's cornfield, if you recall, my Finder ran neck and neck with the count's Tormentor, while your Flyer was half a mile behind.

CHUBUKOV. He was behind because the count's man had taken the whip to him.

LOMOV. Yes, and for good reason! All the other dogs were after a fox — your Flyer was after a sheep!

CHUBUKOV. That's not true! My dear good man, I have a very short fuse, so let's bring this discussion to an end. The count's man took the whip to him because everyone's jealous of their neighbour's dog. They all hate everyone else! You're not beyond reproach yourself, sir! As soon as you notice that someone's dog is better than your Finder you immediately start all this kind of thing . . . I haven't forgotten, you know!

LOMOV. I haven't forgotten, either!

NATALYA STEPANOVNA. (*mimics him*) I haven't forgotten, either . . . And what is it *you* haven't forgotten?

LOMOV.   Palpitations . . . Leg's   gone   again . . . Can't move . . .

NATALYA STEPANOVNA. (*mimics him*) Palpitations . . . Fine one you are to go hunting! You should be in bed over the kitchen stove, like someone's grandfather! You should be squashing cockroaches, not hunting foxes! Palpitations . . .

CHUBUKOV. Yes! Hunting, indeed! You should be sitting at home with these palpitations of yours, not running round on top of a horse. It's not as if you actually hunted — all you go for is to pick quarrels and get in the way of other people's dogs, et cetera et cetera. I have a very short fuse, so let's leave it at that. A hunter! You've not a hunter!

LOMOV. And you think you're a hunter, do you? All you go for is to suck up to the count and get on with your scheming! Oh, my heart! You . . . schemer

CHUBUKOV. What? A schemer, sir? Me, sir? (*Shouts.*) Hold your tongue, sir!

LOMOV. Schemer!

CHUBUKOV. You young puppy!

LOMOV. You old rat! You Jesuit!

CHUBUKOV. Hold your tongue, or I'll shoot you like a partridge! You blatherskite!

LOMOV. Everyone knows—oh, my heart!—your poor wife used to beat you . . . My leg . . . my head . . . my vision's gone . . . I can't stand up!

CHUBUKOV. Your housekeeper's got you on a piece of string!

LOMOV. Go on, go on, go on . . . I'm having a heart attack! My shoulder's missing! Where's my shoulder . . . ? I'm dying! (*Falls into an armchair.*) Doctor! Get a doctor! (*Faints.*)

CHUBUKOV. Little whippersnapper! Little milksop! Little blatherskite! I feel faint. (*Drinks water.*) I'm going to faint!

NATALYA STEPANOVNA. A hunter! Don't make me laugh! You can't even sit on a horse! (*To her father.*) Papa! What's wrong with him? Papa—look at him! (*Screams.*) He's dead!

CHUBUKOV. I'm going to faint! I can't breathe! Air, give me some air!

NATALYA STEPANOVNA. He's dead! (*Pulls at LOMOV's sleeve.*) Ivan Vasilyevich! Ivan Vasilyevich! What have we done? He's dead! (*Falls into an armchair.*) A doctor! Fetch a doctor! (*Has hysterics.*)

CHUBUKOV. What? What? What's the matter with you?

NATALYA STEPANOVNA. (*moans*) He's dead . . . dead . . . !

CHUBUKOV. Who's dead? (*Looks at LOMOV.*) So he is! Heavens above! Water! Fetch a doctor! (*Lifts a glass to LOMOV's lips.*) Come on, have a drink . . . He's not drinking . . . He's dead, then, and all the rest of

it . . . Oh, did any man have such wretched luck as me?
Why don't I put a bullet through my head? How have I
come all this way in life without cutting my throat? What
am I waiting for? Give me a knife! Give me a pistol! (*He
gestures with the glass, which splashes water over
LOMOV, who stirs.*) He's coming round!

LOMOV. Spots . . . Mist . . . Where am I?

CHUBUKOV. For heaven's sake, just marry her, and get
it over with! She says yes! (*Joins LOMOV's and his
daughter's hands.*) The answer's yes, and all the rest of it!
I give you my blessing, et cetera et cetera. Just leave me in
peace, that's all I ask!

LOMOV. Um? What? (*Gets up.*) Who?

CHUBUKOV. She said yes! All right? Give her a kiss
and . . . and to hell with it!

NATALYA STEPANOVNA. (*moans*) He's
alive . . . Yes, yes, I'm saying yes.

CHUBUKOV. Give her a kiss, then!

LOMOV. Who—her? (*Kisses NATALYA STEPAN-
OVNA.*) Oh, very nice . . . I'm sorry—what's all this
about? Oh, yes, I know . . . My heart . . . All these
spots . . . No, I'm very happy . . . (*Kisses her hand.*)
Leg's gone . . .

NATALYA STEPANOVNA. I'm . . . yes, very happy,
too.

CHUBUKOV. That's a load off my
mind . . . Champagne!

(*Enter all the SERVANTS in celebratory mood, with
champagne and glasses, and mugs for themselves.
They raise them to the happy couple in a babble of
congratulations.*)

NATALYA STEPANOVNA. (*To LOMOV, good-

humouredly) Anyway, you can admit it now. Flyer's a better dog than Finder.

LOMOV. (*obstinately*) No, he's not!

NATALYA STEPANOVNA. Yes, he is!

CHUBUKOV. The start of another happy marriage!

LOMOV. He's not a better dog!

NATALYA STEPANOVNA. He is! He is! He is!

CHUBUKOV. (*struggling to shout them down*) Champagne! Champagne! Champagne!

Curtain

To reduce the evening to a workable length when the original production of *The Sneeze* was mounted, one play, *Plots* (adapted from a short story with the same title) was dropped. I am including it here in case it would suit the purposes of a different company better to substitute it for one of the other plays. – MF.

Plots

The bedroom of DR SHELESTOV, a general practi-
tioner in a provincial town. The room is empty. Sud-
denly the door is flung open, and DR SHELESTOV,
dressed in his somewhat shabby everyday three-
piece working suit, stalks languidly into the room.
He raises his hand to dismiss the instant imaginary
uproar that his entry has caused.

SHELESTOV. No . . . No . . . I have nothing to
say . . . You may shout until you are black in the face,
gentlemen — I have not come here tonight to defend
myself. (*He goes to the wardrobe, which has a full-length*
mirror in the door, and examines himself while he lan-
guidly raises his hand for silence again.) I have not come
here tonight to make speeches. I have no intention of
trying to justify my behaviour to this meeting . . . (*He*
stops, dissatisfied, and takes his only other suit out of the
wardrobe. Without taking it off its hanger he holds it up
in front of himself and repeats the gesture in front of the
mirror.) I should not deign to give an account of myself
to this Association . . . (*He stops again, takes a tie off*
the rack, and holds it up with the suit.) I should not
demean myself by defending my conduct at this meeting, which was summoned by the Committee quite un-
constitutionally, without regard to its own rules and pro-
cedures . . . (*He stops again, still dissatisfied, then*
hunts around the room for something else.) Yes, I *have*
read what it says on the agenda . . . 'Item 3. Discussion
of the incident on the second of October.' Hon. members
may discuss the incident on the second of October, if
they choose, until their heads fall off, but I shall maintain
a dignified silence until such time as . . . (*He finds*

102

what he is looking for—his spare pair of shoes. He looks at himself in the mirror again, holding up the suit and tie, with the shoes standing on the floor in front of his feet. He is encouraged by what he sees.) Very well, gentlemen . . . I see that I am reluctantly compelled to speak out. I have come to this meeting quite unprepared, so you will forgive me if my speech is not as polished as I could wish. Let us begin at the beginning . . . (*He hooks the suit up ready to put it on, and begins decisively to take off his jacket and tie.*) The facts of the case are these. Some of my esteemed fellow-doctors have accused me of unprofessional conduct. They allege that my behaviour during joint consultations at our surgery here has left something to be desired, and they demand an explanation. Very well. Let no one say afterwards that this confrontation was of my seeking. Now . . . (*He leans easily against the back of a chair, and folds his arms.*) do not dispute that I have on occasion raised my voice during consultations . . . *He stops and unfolds his arms. He takes his watch out of his waistcoat-pocket, and swings it negligently back and forth on its chain as he repeats the point.*) I accept that I have on occasion raised my voice during consultations and interrupted my learned colleagues . . . (*The watch fails to create the right impression. He puts it back, and takes out a silver pencil instead, which he taps negligently against his palm.*) I have, I agree, on occasion interrupted my learning colleagues in the presence of members of the public . . . (*The pencil is wrong. He puts it away, and goes back to folded arms.*) I did on one occasion, I admit, say to a patient in the presence of his relatives and other doctors: 'Which damned fool prescribed you opium?' There have been very few consultations, I agree, that we have got through without some kind of scene. Why should this be? The answer is very simple. Because I am perpetually amazed at my colleagues' ignorance. There are thirty-two doctors in this town, and most of them know slightly less about their subject than a first-year medical student! (*He takes off his waistcoat while his audience absorbs this piece of plain speaking.*) I have no wish to name names, but it is no secret, I think, that our distinguished colleague Dr von Braun stuck his probe through a certain patient's oesophagus . . . ! (*He turns to listen with disdain to something being said from another quarter.*) I shall treat Dr von Braun's ridiculous counter-allegation with the contempt it deserves. (*He unlaces his shoes as he talks.*) Nor is it any secret that our distinguished colleague Dr Weiss mistook a floating kidney for an abcess, and attempted to lance it, with prompt and fatal consequences. One of our esteemed Ukrainian members set out to remove the big toenail from his patient's left foot . . . (*He pulls off his left shoe.*) . . . and removed the perfectly healthy nail from his right foot instead . . . (*He pulls off his right shoe, and uses it to gesture with as he proceeds.*) Nor can I resist mentioning the time when a certain learned gentleman with an Armenian surname . . . Good evening, sir . . . syringed a patient's Eustachean tubes with such enthusiasm that it burst both his eardrums. I might remind you that it was this same gentleman who once dislocated a patient's jaw while he was pulling a tooth, and who declined to put it right until the patient had agreed to pay him an extra five rubles. It is common knowledge in this Association, I think, that the wife of our learned Chairman lives with our no less learned but somewhat younger Secretary. I see that I have shifted imperceptibly from medical to ethical shortcomings. (*He takes his trousers off.*) Well, so be it. The question of

ethics in this Association is a sore one. Again, I have no
intention of naming names, but I must in all fairness
point out that our distinguished colleague Dr Puzyrkov
has been going round telling everyone that it was not the
Secretary who was living with the Chairman's wife — it
was *me*! And this from Dr Puzyrkov — whom I caught
last year in a compromising situation with Dr Schnaubisch's wife! (*He calmly begins to put on the trousers of
the suit he has laid out while the meeting digests this
piece of information. When he is ready he holds up his
hand to silence the uproar.*) Nor is it any coincidence . . . (*He waits for silence, hand upraised.*) Nor is
it any coincidence that I have had occasion to mention
the name of Herr Doktor Schnaubisch today in the same
connection as Herr Doktor von Braun and Herr Doktor
Weiss. The affairs of this Association are in the hands of a
small and closely-knit cabal! Yes, gentlemen — they're
all in it together! I see from the agenda that the next item
is the re-election of the Chairman for the coming year. I
feel obliged to inform you, before you cast your votes,
that this Chairman of yours, Herr Doktor Gustav Gustavovich Prechtel, practises homeopathy on the quiet, and
that he is in the pay of the Prussian Government! Yes,
gentlemen — the Chairman of the District Medical Association is a Prussian spy! (*He puts on the new waistcoat
and tie, looking at himself with quiet satisfaction in the
mirror, and brushing aside the entreaties of people
around him.*) No, no . . . I have no intention of standing for election myself . . . No . . . No . . . Well,
only if Dr Prechtel and Dr von Braun apologise to me for
the incident on the second of October . . . (*He gra-
ciously inclines his head to listen.*) *Thank* you. I think I
know how to be magnanimous . . . Very well, then —
if you insist, I am prepared to let my name go for-

ward . . . (*He puts on his jacket. He is ready. He takes a last look at himself in the mirror, then steps up on to the chair, smiling and trying to stem the cheering and applause.*) Thank you, gentlemen! I am very gratified and honoured by such . . . thank you . . . thank you . . . by such an overwhelming vote of confidence. My first task as your new Chairman . . . Thank you . . . My first task will be to cleanse the Augean stables. So, any distinguished members of this Association with Armenian surnames — out! All our esteemed colleagues of the Hebraic persuasion — out! My supporters and I will ensure that this Association is purged of every single member of the old gang. And I pledge myself to the following programme:

1. A fresh coat of paint for our premises.
2. A No Smoking sign on the wall.
3. A ban on all operations unless performed under my personal supervision; and
4. The printing of visiting-cards with the words 'Chairman of the Local Medical Association' after my name.

(*He raises his arms to acknowledge the enthusiasm of the crowd, but at that moment the clock in the hall outside begins to strike seven. As it does so, all SHELESTOV's elation drains out of him. He slowly lowers his arms and gets off the chair. He looks at himself dubiously in the mirror. He has shrunk; his suit no longer fits him. He tries to drag it closer to the shape of his body, but it is a disaster.*) No, no, no! (*He tears off the jacket, and puts back the shabby jacket he took off. It doesn't go with the rest of the suit. He rips open his flies and tries to drag down his trousers, but they are held up by braces. He starts to tear off the jacket to get at the braces, then realises he will have to undo all the waistcoat buttons, and instead frantically undoes the front buttons of the braces. He drags the trousers down around his ankles. But they won't come off over his shoes. He glances at his watch in a panic, then drags the trousers up again and does up the flies. He looks at himself wretchedly in the mirror. The jacket does not go with the trousers — and now the trousers keep sagging! He shouts madly at the reflection of them in the mirror.)* Damn you! You're all in this together! *(He turns and goes to the door, his braces still hanging down unnoticed at the back of his sagging trousers.)*

Curtain.

The Pronunciation of the Names

The following is an approximate practical guide. In general, all stressed a's are pronounced as in 'far' (the sound is indicated below by 'aa') and all stressed o's as in 'more' (they are written below as 'aw'). All unstressed a's and o's are thrown away and slurred. The u's are pronounced as in 'crude'; they are shown below as 'oo'. A y at the beginning of a syllable, in front of another vowel, is pronounced as a consonant (i.e., as in 'yellow', not as in 'sky').

Drama

Pavel Vasilyevich — P*aa*vyel Va*seel*yeveech
Murashkina — Moo*raash*keena
Luka — *Look*a

Tarakanov — Tara*kaan*ov
Bogatov — Bo*gaat*ov
Bogatova — Bo*gaat*ova
Sasha — *Saash*a
Dasha — *Daash*a
Anna Sergeyevna — *Aan*na Ser*gay*evna
Marya Andreyevna — *Maar*ya An*dray*evna
Valentin Ivanovich — Valen*teen* Ee*vaan*oveech

The Alien Corn

Kamyshev — Kami*shawff*
Misha — *Meesh*a

The Sneeze

Brizzhalov — Breez-*zhaal*-ov
Chervyakov — Chairvya*kawf*

The Bear

Popova (Yelena Ivanovna) — *Pawp*ova (Yel*yay*na
  Ee*vaan*ovna)
Smirnov (Grigory Stepanovich) — Smeer*nawf* (Gree-
  *gawr*i Ste*paan*oveech)
Luka — *Look*a
Dasha — *Daash*a
Gruzdyov — Groozd*yawf*
Korchagin — Kor*chaag*een
Kuritzin — *Koor*itzin
Matuzov — Ma*tooz*ov
Nikolai — Neeko*lie*
Pelageya — Pela*gaya*
Semyon — Sem*yawn*
Vlasov — *Vlaas*ov
Yaroshevich — Yaro*shay*veech

The Evils of Tobacco

Nyukhin — *Nyookh*een
Natalya Semyonovna — Na*taal*ya Sem*yawn*ovna

The Inspector-General

Pyotr Pavlovich Posudin — Pyotr *Paav*loveech
  Po*sood*een
Nastasya Ivanovna — Nas*taas*ya Ee*vaan*ovna
Ludmila Semyonovna — Lood*meel*a Se*yawn*ovna
Kachalnaya — Ka*chal*naya

Swan Song

Svetlovidov (Vasily Vasilich) — Svetlo*veed*ov (Va*see*li
  Va*seel*eech)
Nikita Ivanich (Nikitushka) — Nee*keet*a
  Ee*vaan*eech (Nee*keet*ooshka)

Petrushka — Pe*troosh*ka
Yegorka — Ye*gawr*ka

The Proposal

Chubukov (Stepan Stepanovich) — Chooboo*kawf* (Ste-*paan* Ste*paan*oveech)
Natalya Stepaanovna — Na*tal*ya Ste*paan*ovna
Lomov (Ivan Vasilyevich) — *Lawm*ov (Ee*vaan* Va-*seel*yeveech)
Maruskin — Ma*roos*kin

Plots

Shelestov — *Shel*estov
Puzyrkov — Poozir*kawf*
Gustavovich — Goo*staav*oveech

Other Publications for Your Interest

BENEFACTORS
(LITTLE THEATRE—COMIC DRAMA)

By MICHAEL FRAYN

2 men, 2 women—Interior

Do not expect another *Noises Off*; here the multi-talented Mr. Frayn has more on his mind than Just Plain Fun. *Benefactors*, a long-running Broadway and London hit, is about doing good and do-gooding (not the same) and about the way the world changes outside your control just when you are trying to change it yourself. The story concerns an architect who has the sixties notion that if you give people good environments they will be good people. But, given a South London development to design, he is forced by town planners to go for a high-rise, characterless scheme. No sooner does he begin to believe in this scheme than the fashion for high rises goes bust. ". . . one of the subtlest plays Broadway has seen in years, by one of the most extraordinary writers of the English-speaking theater . . . more political than most political plays, more intimate than most intimate plays and wiser than almost any play around today."—Newsweek. ". . . a fine . . . very good play . . . A Christmas present for theatergoers."—WABC-TV. ". . . a high point of the theater season . . . rare wit and intelligence."—Wall Street Journal. ". . . fascinating and astonishing play . . ."—N.Y. Daily News. ". . . dazzling and devastating play . . ."—N.Y. Times. ". . . a tour de force . . . simultaneously compelling and alienating . . ."—Christian Science Monitor.   (#3980)

PACK OF LIES
(LITTLE THEATRE—DRAMA)

By HUGH WHITEMORE

3 men, 5 women—Combination interior

Bob and Barbara Jackson are a nice middle-aged English couple. Their best friends are their neighbors, Helen and Peter Kroger, who are Canadian. All is blissful in the protected, contained little world of the Jacksons; until, that is, a detective from Scotland Yard asks if his organization may use the Jackson's house as an observation station to try and foil a Soviet spy ring operating in the area. Being Good Citizens the Jacksons oblige, though they become progressively more and more put out as Scotland Yard's demands on them increase. They are really put to the test when the detective reveals to them that the spies are, in fact, their best friends the Krogers. Scotland Yard asks the Jacksons to cooperate with them to trap the spies, which really puts the Jacksons on the horns of a dilemma. Do they have the right to "betray" their friends? "This is a play about the morality of lying, not the theatrics of espionage, and, in Mr. Whitemore's view, lying is a virulent disease that saps patriots and traitors alike of their humanity."—N.Y. Times. "A crackling melodrama."—Wall St. Journal. "Absolutely engrossing . . . an evening of dynamic theatre."—N.Y. Post. "A superior British drama."—Chr. Sci. Mon.   (#18154)

Other Publications for Your Interest

SEASCAPE WITH SHARKS AND DANCER
(LITTLE THEATRE—DRAMA)

By DON NIGRO

1 man, 1 woman—Interior

This is a fine new play by an author of great talent and promise. We are very glad to be introducing Mr. Nigro's work to a wide audience with *Seascape With Sharks and Dancer*, which comes directly from a sold-out, critically acclaimed production at the world-famous Oregon Shakespeare Festival. The play is set in a beach bungalow. The young man who lives there has pulled a lost young woman from the ocean. Soon, she finds herself trapped in his life and torn between her need to come to rest somewhere and her certainty that all human relationships turn eventually into nightmares. The struggle between his tolerant and gently ironic approach to life and her strategy of suspicion and attack becomes a kind of war about love and creation which neither can afford to lose. In other words, this is quite an offbeat, wonderful love story. We would like to point out that the play also contains a wealth of excellent *monologue* and *scene material*.   (#21060)

GOD'S SPIES
(COMEDY)

By DON NIGRO

1 man, 2 women—Interior

This is a truly hilarious send-up of "Christian" television programming by a talented new playwright of wit and imagination. We are "on the air" with one of those talk shows where people are interviewed about their religious conversions, offering testimonials of their faith up to God and the Moral Majority. The first person interview by stalwart Dale Clabby is Calvin Stringer, who discourses on devil worship in popular music. Next comes young Wendy Trumpy, who claims to have talked to God in a belfry. Her testimonial, though, is hardly what Dale expected . . . Published with *Crossing the Bar*.   (#9643)

CROSSING THE BAR
(COMEDY)

By DON NIGRO

1 man, 2 women—Interior

Two women sit in a funeral parlor with the corpse of a recently-deceased loved one, saying things like "Doesn't he look like himself", when the corpse sits up, asking for someone named Betty. Who is this Betty, they wonder? God certainly works in mysterious ways . . . Published with *God's Spies*.   (#5935)